AF488038

Easy Linux Device Driver, Second Edition

Mahesh Sambhaji Jadhav.

Book may be purchased for educational, business or sales promotional use.

Print editions and online editions of book are also available with title as Easy Linux Device Driver.

Version History:

First Edition: 13 March 2014

Second Edition: 13 July 2014

Publishers & Distributors:

HighTechEasy Publishing.

Address: B-201, Royal Residency, Balewadi, Pune, India. 411045.

Phone: +91 9421359187

Email: hightecheasypub@gmail.com

Blog: www.hightecheasy.wordpress.com

Easy Linux Device Driver
Index

1. Introduction of Linux   **11**

- Advantages of Linux
- History of Linux
- Architecture of Linux
- Definitions

2. Ubuntu installation   **22**

- Ubuntu Installation Steps
- User Interface Difference
- About KNOPPIX
- Important links

3. Terminal: Soul of Linux   **32**

- Creating Root account
- Terminal Commands
- Virtual Editor Commands

4. Linux Kernel   **43**

- Linux Kernel Internals
- Kernel Space and User space

5. Device Driver   **50**

- Place of Driver in System

- Device Driver working
- Characteristics of Device Driver
- Module Commands

6. Hello World Program   **59**

- pre-settings
- Write Program
- Printk function
- Makefile
- Run program

7. Parameter passing   **74**

- Parameter passing program
- Parameter Array

8. Process related program   **84**

- Process related program

9. Character Device Driver   **90**

- Major and Minor number
- API to registers a device
- Program to show device number

10. Character Driver File Operations   **98**

- File operation program.
- Include .h header
- Functions in module.h file
- Important code snippets
- Summary of file operations

11. PCI Device Driver   **113**

- Direct Memory Access
- Module Device Table
- Code for Basic Device Driver
- Important code snippets

12. USB Device Driver Fundamentals   **130**

- Architecture of USB device driver
- USB Device Driver program

13. Structure of USB Device Driver   **141**

- Parts of USB end points
- Important features
- USB information Driver

14. USB device Driver File Operations   **153**

- Using URB
- Simple data transfer
- Program to read and write
- Important code snippets
- Gadget Driver

15. Complete USB Device Driver Program   **174**

- Skeleton Driver Program

16. Special USB 3.0   **205**

- USB 3.0 Port connection
- Bulk endpoint streaming
- Stream ID

17. Device Driver Lock   **211**

- Mutual Exclusion
- Semaphore
- Spin Lock

18. Display Device Driver   **217**

- Frame buffer concept
- Framebuffer Data Structure
- Check and set Parameter
- Accelerated Method
- Display Driver summary

19. Memory Allocation   **233**

- Kmalloc
- Vmalloc
- Ioremap

20. Interrupt Handling   **244**

- interrupt registration
- Proc interface
- Path of interrupt
- Programming Tips
- Softirqs, Tasklets, Work Queues

21. I/O Control   **256**

- Introducing ioctl
- Prototype
- Stepwise execution of ioctl

22. Sample Device Driver   **262**

- Complete memory Driver
- Complete Parallel Port Driver

23. Device Driver Debugging   **293**

- Data Display Debugger
- Graphical Display Debugger
- Kernel Graphical Debugger

Appendix I   **299**

- Exported Symbols
- Kobjects, Ksets, and Subsystems
- DMA I/O

Bibliography   **307**

Preface

Welcome to world of simplicity!!

Book is especially designed for those who want to understand Linux device driver programming in easy and simple way along with Linux fundamental's and Linux internals.

Book gives exactly what Linux Device Driver developer wants to kick start of driver programming.

References of many great books, magazines, experiments by the author, internet sources, Linux community reference materials make this book a unique one.

Primary objective of this book is to make Linux programing simple to learn, easy to adopt and an efficient reference guide for beginners. Programing with help of this User guide will be delightful.

It is my pleasure to dedicate this book to Linux community, my friends and family. Collecting all scattered material from sea of Linux will surely be helpful to open source community.

I would welcome and appreciate readers to send their valuable views and feedback to make the book more useful. I would surely incorporate all the valuable suggestions in the next edition.

Friends, Its time to go through the steps and become Linux Device Driver Experts!!

All The Best!! And I am with you. ☺

-Mahesh Sambhaji Jadhav

Chapter 1
Introduction to Linux

Linux is the most popular open source operating system.

All of us are quite familiar with windows operating system. Footprints of windows operating system can be seen at every doorsteps. UNIX, another operating system emerged prior to windows operating system and can be called as mother of all Linux operating system.

Linux is a famous variant of Unix operating system. Linux become so popular that many times Linux word gets used as substitute of UNIX.

Do you know?

Even today linux is used in our day to day life. From large super computer computing gigabites of data and huge server holding tremendous data along with many small handheld devices and electronic equipments uses linux as their operating system.

Yes...It may be the legendary I-os in I-phone or fastest growing operating system Android in smart phone! All these mobile operating systems are actually based on Linux.They uses linux kernel variant inside operating system☺.

Linux quickly evolved from a single-person project to a world-wide development project involving thousands of developers.

Linux device driver made easy.

Advantages of Linux operating System:

- Linux is free to use and distribute.

- Support is free through online help sites, blogs and forums.

- It is very reliable than most of the other operating systems with very few crashes.

- A huge amount of free open source software has been developed for it.

- It is very resistant to malware such as spyware, adware and viruses.

- Linux runs in a wide variety of machines.

- Linux offers greater security for sensitive applications as the source code is visible and the 'backdoors' are easily spotted.

- Linux offers a high degree of flexibility in configuration.

- Significant customization is possible without modifying the source code.

History of Linux:

Significant development of UNIX began in 1969 at Bell laboratories in the USA. Ken Thompson wrote first version in assembler. To get a better idea of what interfaces and drivers would be needed; he wrote the game 'space Travel' along with Dennis Richie.

Ken and Dennis soon worked out which component is used in operating system and how the whole thing should be organized. During 1970 and 1974 they re-wrote the heart of operating system from scratch using C programing language, which also includes C compiler. After some time AT&T started selling UNIX operating system.

Richard Stallman at MIT, USA put a massive effort in GNU in order to re-implement everything to create 100% free operating system.

At around same time Linus Torvalds bought his first x_86 computer and wrote terminal program on it.

As he worked on this terminal, Linus saw that it was becoming more and more like operating system itself.

Open source community quickly realized that Linus Torvald's kernel was the missing element in Richard Stallman's GNU project.

On 5 October 1991 Linus Torvalds released first time Linux operating system to the world, which became popular over the decade. "Linux: Emulator of UNIX" was a college level project performed by Linus. However, after fabulous enhancements Linux become greatest ever operating system in the world.

Ubuntu, Red Hat, Suse, Fedora are the famous distribution variant of Linux. Linux kernel and application developers around the world perform new changes in the source code of Linux to enhance the operating system.

[Click the link www.linux.org to reach the home of Linux.]

The prerequisite to learn Linux operating system internals

Learning Linux operating system is simple if one has used windows.

Fundamental Architecture of Linux:

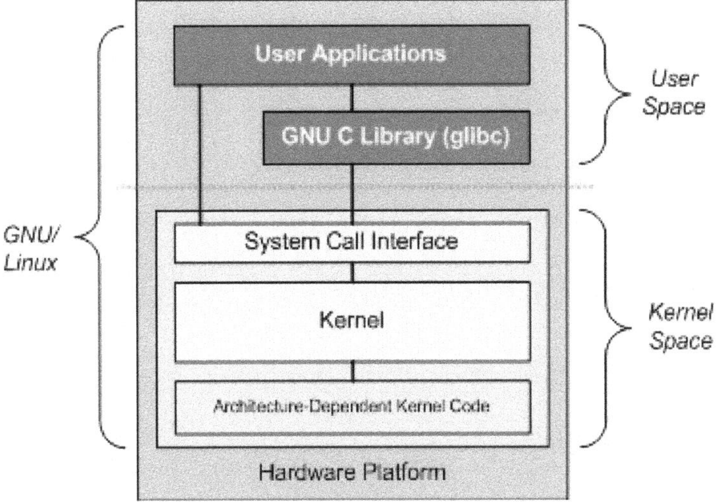

At the top is the user or application, space. This is where the user applications are executed. Kernel space for Linux kernel is below the user space.

GNU C Library (glibc) provides the system call interface that connects to the kernel and provides the mechanism to transition between the user-space application and the kernel.

Linux kernel can be further divided into three gross levels. At the top is the system call interface, which implements the basic functions such as read and write.

Below the system call interface is the kernel code, which can be more accurately defined as the architecture-independent kernel code. This code is common to all of the processor architectures supported by Linux.

Below this is the architecture-dependent code, which is more commonly called a BSP (Board Support Package). This code serves as the processor and platform-specific code for the given architecture.

Definitions:

✓ Linux kernel is a type of monolithic kernel. Monolithic kernel is a single large processes running entirely in a single address space. All kernel services exist and execute in kernel address space. The kernel can invoke functions directly. In short, entire operating system works in kernel space and is alone in supervisor mode.

✓ Device drivers are either integrated directly with the kernel or added as modules while the system is running.

✓ A bootloader is a program which is executed by the computer when it is first turned on, and loads the Linux kernel into memory.

✓ An init program is first process launched by the Linux kernel, and is at the root of the process tree. It starts processes such as system services and login prompts.

✓ Software libraries containing code can be used by running processes. The most commonly used software library on Linux systems is the GNU C Library.

Basic things needed for device driver programming are learnt from this book to quickly move in to device driver programming.

Simple and step wise approach is used to learn and understand linux device driver programming.

Chapter 2
Ubuntu Installation

Installation of Linux Operating system on the computer.

Ubuntu is the variant of Linux and is getting popular among the youths due to crazy features and competitive user interface.

It is one of the best operating system for those who want to transfer from windows experience to Linux experience.

Ubuntu has user interface close to windows but internally base of Ubuntu is Linux.

Crazy thing about Linux is that its source code is completely open. Lots of cool stuff can be done inside the code and enhance Linux operating system.

The main advantage of Ubuntu is that the creators and developers made this distribution easy to install, maintain and use.

Ubuntu has a very large community, giving users much better support than some other GNU/Linux distributions.

Linux gives great opportunity to create and customize the operating system. Developing one's own customized operating system is not that easy and it needs to experiment the stuff, with passion and interest. ELDD will make the startup smooth.

Steps to Install Ubuntu OS:

- Turn on your computer.
- Boot the system in windows os.
- Windows may be windows xp, windows 7 or windows 8 anything will be fine.
- Open the browser internet explorer or crome or Firefox and open below link of Ubuntu.

  Link: www.ubuntu.com/download

Ubuntu can be installed on the computer without deleting the data in system so that it can be used along with windows as per the need.

On Ubuntu website page, windows installer for Ubuntu can be found, which will work just like any other installer in windows without any trouble.

Above screenshot shows Ubuntu desktop installer.

Click on the link of windows installer.

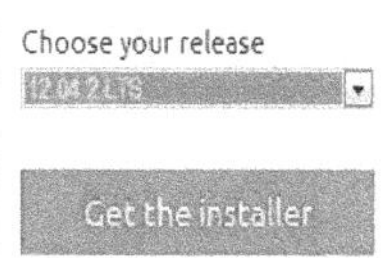

From dropdown box choose the version which is required to be installed. Click on get Installer button to download installer.exe

Note: Choose latest version of Ubuntu from release dropdown. LST version stands for long time support version of Ubuntu which is stable version and for such version we can get long time support from Ubuntu.

Then you can see donation pop up window click on "Not now, take me to the download "link. (If you want to donate some amount to Ubuntu organization then feel free to do so.)

A message pops up indicating operating system installer is ready to download. Run that setup or save on your system and start installation of Ubuntu operating system using this installer.

During that phase, provide Username and password for system. Also see a window shown below where one can enter more details and provide how much memory space to be provided for Ubuntu.

Fill up all the data in window and click on Install button. It will kick off installation further.

The system will restart for twice or thrice at time of installation and then finally it shows log in window of Ubuntu.

Then give username and password and Enter in to Ubuntu.

System will sing a sweet musical sound and one get entered in to world of Linux.

It's that much simple..!!!

Tips for using Ubuntu and windows together on single system:

After system restart two options can be seen on boot screen to choose operating system.

Enter the operating system as Ubuntu to boot for this time.

User Interface Difference between Ubuntu and windows:

We can observe that as windows have task bar on lower bottom, Ubuntu have task bar on upper side. On top right side of task bar you can find options for shut down or restart.

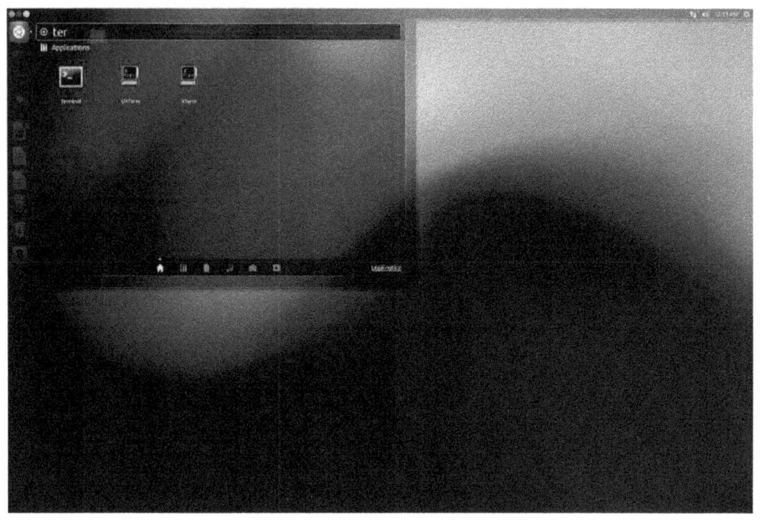

[Ubuntu Operating System user Interface]

In windows when any window is opened on the screen; application window contains option for minimize, maximize or close the window on upper right but on Ubuntu. We can see same options on upper left.

On left hand side of screen we can see options regarding applications for Ubuntu.

On upper left corner of window a button can be observed which will work similar to as start button of windows. By using this button the search required applications. Click on searched options to open that application.

Start playing with Ubuntu and you can really enjoy working. It will surely be a joy…and will give the feel of using great legendary operating system.

About KNOPPIX :

KNOPPIX, is an linux operating system based on Debian designed to be run directly from a CD / DVD or a USB flash drive.

It is a bootable Live system on CD or DVD, consisting of a representative collection of GNU/Linux software, automatic hardware detection, and supports for many graphics cards, USB devices and other peripherals.

KNOPPIX can be used as a productive Linux system for the desktop, educational CD and used as a platform for commercial software product demos.

It is not necessary to install anything on a hard disk. Due to on-the-fly decompression, the CD can have up to 2 GB of executable software installed on it.

Link:www.knopper.net/knoppix/index-en.html

Important links regarding Linux:

1]   www.kernel.org : This link will provide complete source code of Linux. One can visit this web site and download complete source code of Linux.

2]   www.lkml.org : This is official mailing list of Linux community. One can contribute in this email discussion or can refer the previous discussion on some topic.

All emails are stored in this web site. One can search required information from this email store.

So with this point we have completed the installation part and basic introduction of Linux.

Chapter 3
Terminal: Soul of Linux

Recently Linux operating system has featured with user interface but from beginning face and frame of Linux was Terminal window; it can be called as the sole of Linux.

Using terminal we can control complete system.

In windows DOS command prompt can be used; similarly, Ubuntu contains terminal window or use.

We will be focusing practical use of Linux in this book. Author has intended to explain Linux internals and programming in easy and simple manner.

The previous chapter discussed the installation of Ubuntu operating system; now turn on the system and boot it in to Ubuntu to start next section.

Click on Ubuntu search box on left top of window and enter "Terminal" in this search box. We can see image of Terminal icon on the window. Click on this icon to launch terminal window.

At a time we can launch multiple Terminal windows and perform different work on different terminal windows. This is really special powerful feature of Linux Terminal window.

One more important thing!! Take any of Linux operating system, its user interface may be different but it's Shell or Terminal always remain identical. Once you go inside the terminal window you can realize no difference between any of Linux variant operating system.

To perform any new changes in system or to install some software's on system you must be system administrator. Therefore, create a root account using terminal window to log in to system as a root user.

Let's learn this basic step first:

Creating Root account:

1) Open Terminal window.
2) Window will show the name logged in to operating system.
3) Then use "sudo passwd root" command.
4) Enter your system password two times when prompted.
5) Enter "su root" command.

6) Enter new password for root account (example: root).

7) After that we get logged in as root account.

8) When we press enter button the username in terminal window will be replaced by root account.

9) From next time when we want to log in by root; just enter "su root" and password and we will be logged-in in to root account.

To understand this procedure see the screenshot of terminal window given below.

```
root@ubuntu: ~
administrator@ubuntu:~$ sudo passwd root
[sudo] password for administrator:
Enter new UNIX password:
Retype new UNIX password:
passwd: password updated successfully
administrator@ubuntu:~$ su root
Password:
root@ubuntu:/home/administrator# cd
root@ubuntu:~#
BOLMJ
```

Now the Terminal is ready for use with full power.

Terminal Commands:

Terminal commands are very helpful in order to control operating system and to perform different operations.

Some of important and useful commands are listed below which we will be using during device driver programming.

Note: Below shell commands are the same for Linux and UNIX.

- ✓ **ls** : This command displays files and directories (folders) where work is going on.

- ✓ **pwd** : This command indicates current directory location.

- ✓ **ps** : This command shows running process in system.

- ✓ **cat** : This command shows content in current file.

- ✓ **cp** : This is used to copy file.

- ✓ **mv** : This command is used to change name of file. mv old name new name.

- ✓ **rm** : This is useful to delete or remove the file.

- ✓ **echo** : This command is used to send arguments.

- ✓ **grep** : It used to search line which contains specific word. grep word file name.

- ✓ **sort** : Using this command file will be read completely then data will be sorted and sorted data will again write into same file.

- ✓ **mkdir** : To create new directory this command will be used.

- ✓ **exit** : To close the terminal window.

[Ref:Unix Made Easy:Tata McGrow-hill:Muster]

Virtual Editor:

To write program in terminal virtual editor is very useful tool. It is also called as VI editor.

The improved version of VI editor is VIM.This is also provided by Linux. The major differential factor in VI modified is that VIM tool shows code in different color format; internally VIM uses VI editor only.

VI editor either works in command mode or insert mode. It means that we can either write the code or run the code at a time but cannot do both things at same time.

In command mode VI editor works in read only mode.

First of all we can give vi file name command and we can go in to editor mode of vi tool.

Then press i button to write in editor.

When the writing is completed press Esc to move back in read only mode.

To move cursor use h, j, k, l buttons.

To find any word from the program use word command and search for that specific word.

To find next word press n and move to location of same word in program.

To quit from editor press Ctrl+Q and then give q! command. If we want to save the file then use wq! command.

To delete any line use dd command.

If we unknowingly delete any row and we want to retrieve same line, use u command.

To delete any letter, go in command mode and move cursor to that letter and press x button.

If we want to start writing from same word then go to that word and press a button, the cursor will move to beginning of that word.

To go directly at particular line of code, give: line number [:112] command and press enter.

To replace any letter we need to move cursor on that letter and press r button and press new letter so that old letter will be replaced by new one.

In this part we learnt about basic command used in VI editor. The learning will surely help you during programming in VI editor.

In addition to these commands, there are many commands in VI editor. Their use will be discussed in further programming exercise.

To know more VI commands click on link given below:

[http://anaturb.net/vim_1.htm]

Tips:

Press up arrow key to see the command just used in terminal.

Instead of typing full file name just type initials of file and press tab button. Full name of file will automatically appears.

We have learnt terminal commands and VI editor commands in this chapter. In the next chapter, focus will be on learning about kernel and device driver, a damn interesting stuff.

vi / vim graphical sheet

Esc
normal mode

motion — moves the cursor, or defines the range for an operator

command — direct action command, if red, it enters insert mode

operator — requires a motion afterwards, operates between cursor & destination

extra — special functions, requires extra input

q. — commands with a dot need a char argument afterwards

bol = beginning of line, eol = end of line,
mk = mark, yank = copy

words: quux{foo, bar, baz} ;
WORDs: quux{foo, bar, baz} ;

Main command line commands ('ex'):
:w (save), :q (quit), :q! (quit w/o saving)
:e f (open file f),
:%s/x/y/g (replace 'x' by 'y' filewide),
:h (help in vim), :new (new file in vim),

Other important commands:
CTRL-R: redo (vim),
CTRL-F/-B: page up/down,
CTRL-E/-Y: scroll line up/down,
CTRL-V: block-visual mode (vim only)

Visual mode:
Move around and type operator to act
on selected region (vim only)

Notes:
(1) use "x before a yank/paste/del command
   to use that register ('clipboard') (x=a..z,")
   (e.g.: "ay$ to copy rest of line to reg 'a')

(2) type in a number before any action
   to repeat it that number of times
   (e.g.: 2p, d2w, 5i, d4j)

(3) duplicate operator to act on current line
   (dd = delete line, >> = indent line)

(4) ZZ to save & quit, ZQ to quit w/o saving

(5) zt: scroll cursor to top,
   zb: bottom, zz: center

(6) gg: top of file (vim only),
   gf: open file under cursor (vim only)

Chapter 4
Linux Kernel

Welcome to chapter 4. Learning fundaments of linux kernel and device driver will proceed from this session. These concepts will be very useful during device driver programming.

Kernel is the core part of Linux operating system. Linux community continuously works together in order to improve the kernel and provides updated features of kernel. User will get new version of kernel with added capabilities and features.

Linux kernel has been written in two language c and assembly programming language.

Kernel assembly code is hardware dependent; comparatively C code is very huge and independent of hardware.

Note: Kernel always runs in kernel space.

Kernel acts as middleware between hardware and user applications. Kernel task data from user and communicates with processor, memory or other devices to execute the task.

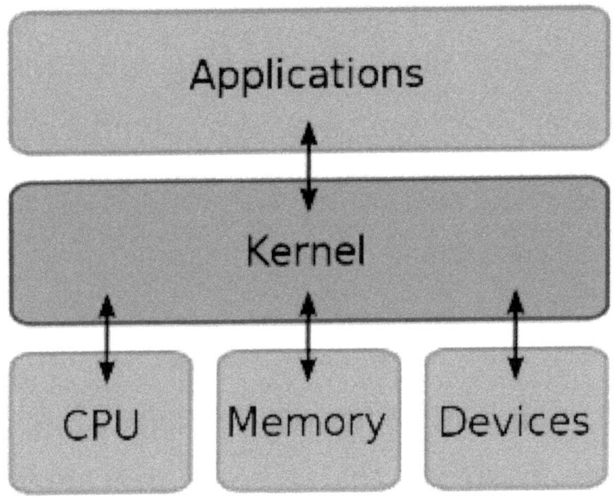

Linux Kernel

Learning of Linux becomes more interesting as we start learning Linux internals.

"As we go deeper and deeper in Linux; complexity increases and is directly proportional to amazing learning experience."

In this chapter we will learn about Linux Insides.

Linux Kernel Internals:

UNIX system is capable of handling several processes at a time. The power feeder behind this is kernel of operating system!

Kernel is a big code which handles important things in operating system like memory, power, process. The important works of kernel are mainly divided in following operations.

Process Management: **Send the processes to** processor, create multiple processes. Run the processes as per the schedule and delete the processes after the task is completed. Process management is performed by kernel in this way.

Memory Management: **To allocate memory to** process, free the memory once used by process. Manage memory using virtual address mechanism.

File System: **File system is the base of Linux.** Linux deals with everything in the form of a file. For example, folder/directory will also be considered as file. The device connected to system will also be a file…Isn't it crazy!

Linux kernel creates a structural layer of file system on top of the hardware. Linux has different file systems for example FAT file system.

Device Control: Device attached to the system has to perform some specific task allocated to it. Specific code called as Device Driver will be executed to perform the specific task.

Kernel system contains some inbuilt driver and others should be installed as per our requirements.

Example: System already have keyboard device driver but when some new speaker is connected to system, we need to install driver of that speaker.

Networking: Identify incoming packets to create network packages and use them for networking related things. Kernel will handle all this.

[Ref:Linux device driver :orelly:Hartman]

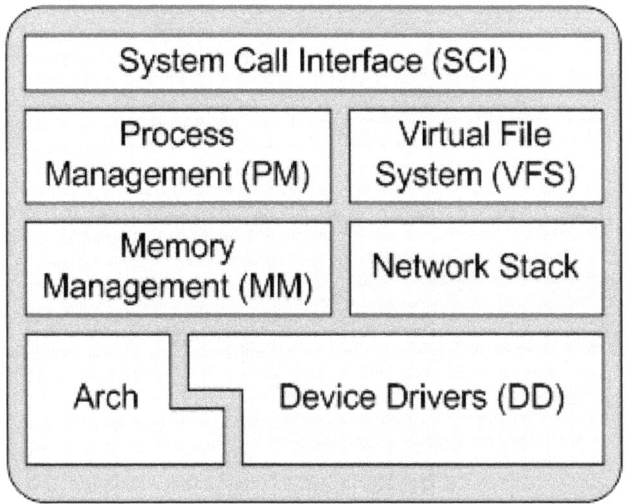

Linux Subsystem Architecture

Note:

A recent advancement of Linux is its use as an operating system for other operating systems (called a hypervisor).

Recently, kernel was modified and the new system is called the Kernel-based Virtual Machine (KVM). This modification enabled a new interface to user space that allows other operating systems to run above the KVM-enabled kernel.

Kernel Space and User space:

User Space: User program, Shell and any other applications are parts of user space. These applications may require interaction with hardware's but direct interaction with hardware's cannot be performed without help of kernel.

Kernel Space: Kernel can directly communicate with hardware. In this process device drivers, driver functions, and system calls help user to interact with the hardware and can perform read or write operation.

In Kernel mode, user will get full access control.

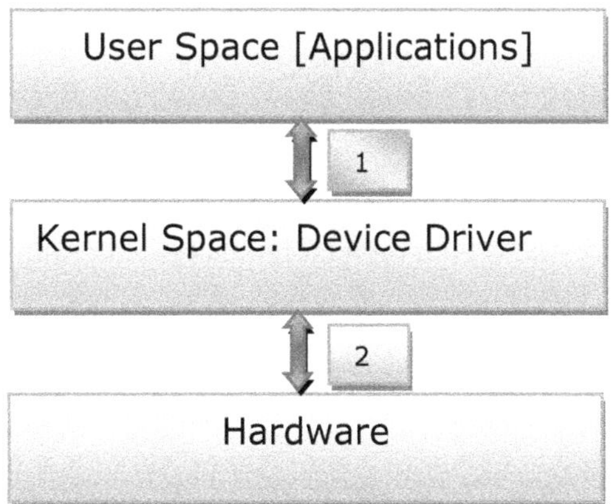

"Device driver works as bridge between applications and hardware."

It's time to jump into Device Driver!

Chapter 5
Device Driver

The purpose of a device driver is to handle requests made by the kernel for particular type of device. Device driver acts as a well-defined and consistent interface for the kernel to make requests to hardware.

Adding a new device is easier by isolating device-specific code in device drivers and having consistent interface to the kernel.

Kernel Calls a Device Driver in following cases:

> At autoconfiguration time (probe interface) to determine what devices are available and to initialize them.

> To perform I/O operations (open, read, write, close) on the device.

> To handle interrupt requests and special requests through ioctl calls.

> To reinitialize the driver, the device, or when the CPU to device bus is reset.

> To handle requests that result from use of the sysconfig utility (configure, unconfigure, query).

Place of a Device Driver in System:

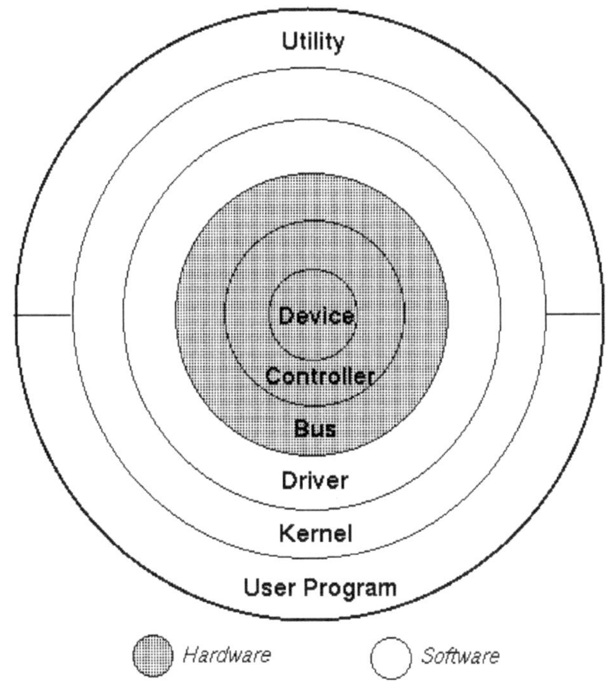

- User program makes calls on the kernel but never calls a device driver directly.
- Kernel runs in supervisor mode and communicates with a device through calls to a device driver.

- Device driver communicates with a device by reading and writing through a bus to peripheral device registers.
- Bus is the data path between the main processor and the device controller.
- Controller is a physical interface to control one or more devices.
- Peripheral device is connected to a controller.

Types of device drivers

Different types of device driver are:

- Character device driver :
    - Use: For byte data transfer.
    - Example: For Line printers and graphics display.
- Block device driver:
    - Use: For storage devices.
    - Example: For Hard disk drives.
- Network packets driver:
    - Use: For packets data transfer.
    - Example: for Network cards.

Device Driver working:

When user connects any device to the system then specific code will define behaviour of that particular device. This code is called as Device driver.

When we connect the device then we need to install the driver for that particular device to be operational.

Some drivers will automatically load as soon as we connect that device to system.

For example when we plug USB pen drive to system, the system automatically detects the device and install the driver for that device and the device starts working.

One of best features of Linux is that user can load or unload the device driver when system is on and is in working state. There is no need to restart the system after driver is loaded or unloaded. Due to this amazing feature, Linux operating system is used in servers which runs for very long duration without restart.

Device driver program is also called as Module as per language of kernel.

Every module works for specific device allocated for it.

We can go to terminal window and give "ls /usr/src/linux/drivers/" command to see if device driver is installed in our system.

Characteristics of Device Driver:

✓ The software that handles or manages a hardware controller is known as a device driver.

✓ The Linux kernel device drivers are shared library of privileged, memory resident, low level hardware handling routines.

✓ Linux's device drivers handle the peculiarities of the devices by managing device specific property.

✓ Device drivers are part of the kernel. A badly written driver may crash the system, possibly corrupting file systems and losing data.

✓ Device drivers provide a standard interface to the Linux kernel. Driver provides both file

I/O and buffer cache interfaces to the kernel.

✓ Device drivers make use of standard kernel services such as memory allocation, interrupt delivery and wait queues to operate.

✓ Most of the Linux device drivers can be loaded on demand as kernel modules when they are needed and unloaded when they are no longer being used. This makes the kernel very adaptable and efficient with the system's resources.

✓ Linux device drivers can be built into the kernel and are configurable when the kernel is compiled.

✓ As the system boots, each device driver is initialized and looks for the hardware devices that it will control. If those devices do not exist then device driver is simply redundant and causes no harm apart from occupying a little of the system's memory.

Module Commands:

Modules are present in kernel object (.ko file) format. We can insert or remove different modules form kernel by using the commands given below:

lsmod: This command shows list of device drivers (modules) available in computer system.

[Note: In further commands, we need to provide module file name along with command.]

insmod **module file name**: We can insert any modules in linux kernel by using this command.

modprobe **module file name**: We can insert the required module along with its related modules in kernel by using this command. When we insert the module then some dependent modules will automatically get inserted in kernel.

rmmod **module file name**: This command is used to remove any module from kernel.

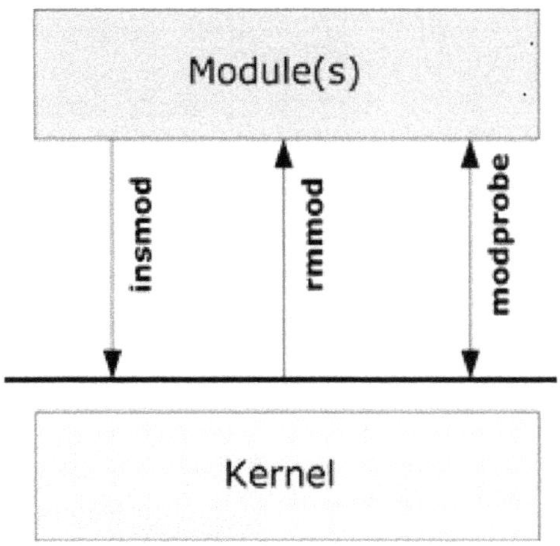

So Guys, in this way we learn all fundamental concepts regarding kernel and device driver. Programming knowledge of these concepts is crucial before starting device driver. In the next chapter we will learn to develop Hello World program of Device driver!

Get Set Go...

Chapter 6
Hello World Program

Start of every programming language happens with a legendary 'Hello World' program. In this chapter we will start with basic Hello world program of Linux device driver. Along with this we will learn about all basic settings and important programming tricks. Reference of this topic is given in further chapters. This is an important chapter to learn.

Device driver program works as a library. It means applications runs using functions provided inside driver drivers.

Device driver program has been written in 'C' language but the major difference is that Driver program does not contain 'main()' function which is used during regular 'C' programs.

Device driver program gets linked and locked by kernel. For this purpose we need to compile our program.

Linux device driver contains constructors and destructor.

Constructor gets called when module loads and destructor will get called when we remove the module using rmmod command.

In device driver program Module init, exit functions take care of this responsibility.

We need to do some pre-settings before starting of Linux device driver program. These include:

- Open terminal window in our Linux computer.

- Login by using root account. [su root].

- [Please refer section 3 to know in detail about creating root account.]

- Then give command as whoami.The output of command will ensures that we are in root account only.

- We will also need to create a directory in Home where we will be storing all our programs. And go to that directory [cd /home/MJ/] I have created directory called as MJ and I will be working in that directory.

- To know in which directory we are, we have to use pwd command. The output of the command will show current working directory.

- If we want to run and write the program using VI editor then give VI hello.c command.

- This command will open hello.c. If it is already present in current directory or create new file if this file does not exist in current directory. After that command we will get in to virtual editor [vi editor]

- Press i button to write in VI editor. VI editor will get into editor mode and we will able to write our program.

- Now copy paste the program given below in VI editor or you can type same program in VI editor.

- Another simple method: Directly open Linux text editor, paste the program in that text editor and save it by using .c extension.

Hello world program:

```c
#include<linux/init.h>
#include<linux/module.h>

MODULE_LICENSE("GPL");

static int hello_init(void)
{
printk(KERN_ALERT "Hello world");
return 0;
}

static void hello_exit(void)
{
printk(KERN_ALERT "Goodby");
}

module_init(hello_init);
module_exit(hello_exit);
```

We will be going through line by line explanation of above program.

At the start of program we need to include some header files. We can see location of included header in our system at /root/include/linux. In this location we can find storage of all .h files.

init.h file gets included to start init process. Almost every Linux device driver we need to include this file.

Code in this file is useful in order to system boot, to insert modules in kernel and to remove modules from kernel. init and exit functions are defined in this file.

1) If you are writing device driver then we must include module.h file in our program. This file contains functions related to modules.

2) MODULE_LICENSE indicates that we are using GPL free license.

3) When module gets loaded in kernel then hello_init function gets called. Therefore, this function is called as initialization function. If this function fails then error code will be returned so this function will never declare as void.

4) **Printk function**: In c programming language we used printf function to display content on the screen. Similarly in Linux kernel programming prink() is used as printing function. Using this function string data will get loaded in kernel log buffer.

Prink function gives special feature to allocate importance of message by attaching tags to the print messages.

Printk function has 8 log levels. These log levels are defined and are inbuilt in kernel.h header file. 8 log levels of printk functions are as given below:

- ✓ KERN_EMERG: This log level is used only for emergency purpose. Example: process stops.
- ✓ KERN_ALERT: To attract the attention.
- ✓ KERN_ERR: To display the error.
- ✓ KERN_CRIT: To tell about critical serious hardware or software problems.
- ✓ KERN_WARNING: Warning message of danger.
- ✓ KERN_NOTICE: Simple notice message.
- ✓ KERN_INFO: Provide Information
- ✓ KERN_DEBUG: To see log messages during debugging.

In above program we have explained to display Hello world message using KERN_ALERT log level.

If any error occurs during this process then return function will return the error code.

5) Use hello_exit function to remove module from kernel. As this function executes, the "GoodBye" message will be displayed in message log records.

6) module_init tells the kernel about function sequence to run after module initialization.

7) After removal of the module from kernel module_exit function tells kernel about the functions to execute.

Once we have written program in VI editor we can enter Ctrl+Q button to quite from editor or we can press Esc button.

 To save the program and then exit use wq! Command.

```
#include<linux/init.h>
#include<linux/module.h>

MODULE_LICENSE("GPL");

static int hello_init(void)
{
        printk(KERN_ALERT "Hello world");
        return 0;
}

static void hello_exit(void)
{
        printk(KERN_ALERT "Goodby");
}

module_init(hello_init);
module_exit(hello_exit);
```

Now as sown in above text editor the program is set to run. To verify the correctness of what we have written; we can open ".c" file in text editor or give cat hello.c in terminal to see the program in read only mode.

Check that everything is all fine. ☺

Makefile:

Compile the code using Make file before running the same. Therefore, create a file name called as MakeFile in the same directory where we placed our entire program.

Alternatively, we need to provide full file path during compilation where Make file is located.

[Note: The word in the file name 'Makefile' is case sensitive. The letter 'M' should be written in capital.]

In front of obj-m, give the name of modules we need to build and then related .o and .ko files will automatically get generated after compilation.

[Note:In MakeFile give the program file name with .o (object) extension and do not use .c extension. Example: hello.o]

Create a **Makefile** with a code mentioned below:

```
obj-m +=hello.o
all:
    make -C /lib/modules/$(shell uname
-r)/build M=$(PWD) modules
clean:
    make -C /lib/modules/$(shell uname
-r)/build M=$(PWD) clean
```

MakeFile Code information:

`shell uname -r` : This command helps to identify which kernel is used in our system. Next line defines the module which will get loaded as part of kernel after loading of the program.

[Note : While writing the above code please remember to press the tab button instead of space button before make word.[Press TAB make].

Run Hello World program:

Go to terminal window and then to file path where we placed our Makefile.

We need to use make command to compile the program. Once we are done with compiling our program we can see supporting files getting generated in the directory.

If the program fails to compile then compiler will provide an error message indicating the line number in which the error occurs.

In this case we need to again run the program by using vi hello.c command and perform the required changes and then quit the program by saving the changes. Again recompile the program using make command.

sudo insmod hello.ko : By using this command we can insert our module in kernel.

To verify if our module is included in kernel, we can go through the kernel log message.

Use dmesg command to view message if logged into kernel logs.

We can see "Hello World" message to see if the function initialization is happening in perfect way.

Using lsmod command we can verify that the newly added module is present in the list of modules in the system.

If we wish to remove our inserted module we need to give the command 'sudo rmmod hello.ko'. After executing this command we can perform dmesg and check for Goodbye message.

[Note : Please note that a module can be inserted only at one time. If we want to insert an updated module again then we need to remove the previously added module first and then insert the new module.]

Please see the below image which indicates the output window after execution of hello world program.

```
root@ubuntu: /home/shri/mjproj
root@ubuntu:/home/shri/mjproj# sudo insmod hello1.ko
root@ubuntu:/home/shri/mjproj# sudo rmmod hello1.ko
root@ubuntu:/home/shri/mjproj# dmesg |tail -5
[  525.848702] Hello world
[  531.628602] Goodby
root@ubuntu:/home/shri/mjproj#
BOLMJ
```

In this chapter we learnt about basic Linux device driver programming.

We have created our own device driver program. Isn't it a proud feeling? Now we will modify our program and explore more to learn further device driver programs.

...till then keep saying hello to Linux world.

[Ref: Linux For You magazine]

Chapter 7
Parameter Passing

In previous topic we learnt about basic hello world program. You would have enjoyed a simple and stepwise process of learning device driver. In this chapter we will go further in order to learn some more basic programs.

Suppose you want to pass some parameters to your device driver then what should be done to pass those parameters? Now we will learn about parameter passing program of the device driver.

Initially, we will pass only single parameter to our module.

Program:

```c
#include<linux/init.h>
#include<linux/module.h>
#include<linux/moduleparam.h>

MODULE_LICENSE("GPL");

int paramTest;
module_param(paramTest,
int,S_IRUSR|S_IWUSR);

static int param_init(void)
{
    printk(KERN_ALERT "Showing the
parameter demo");
    printk(KERN_ALERT "VALUE OF
PARAMTEST IS: %d",paramTest);
    return 0;
}
static void param_exit(void)
{
    printk(KERN_ALERT "Exiting the
parameter demo");
}

module_init(param_init);
module_exit(param_exit);
```

[Ref: Linux For You magazine]

We will include moduleparam as a header file in above program to take the benefit of module parameter related functions.

```
module_param(paraameter name, data type
,permission);
```

Using this format we can provide parameter related information to kernel. It gives information about parameter name, data type of parameter and permisstion given to that parameter.

There are 5 types of permissions: S_IWUSR, S_IRUSR, S_IXUSR, S_IRGRP, S_WGRP

Explanation of each permission will be decoded using below identifiers.

- In this S_I is common header.

- R = Read ,W =Write ,X= Execute.

- USR =User ,GRP =Group

- Using OR '|' (or operation) we can set multiple perissions at a time.

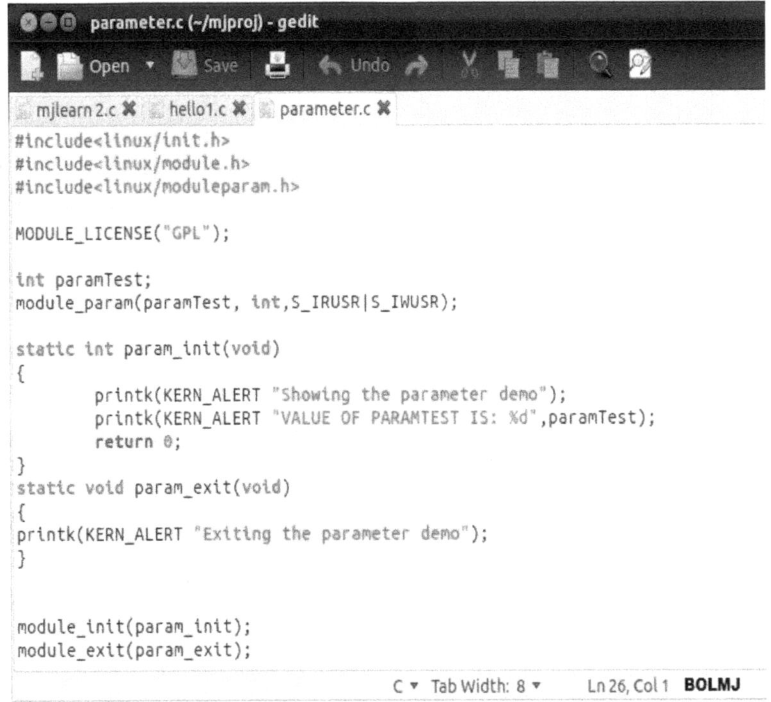

Above screenshot shows how to modify our Hello World program. To run this program we need to perform some steps mentioned below.

In Makefile replace hello.o by our new file name [parameter.o] and save that modified make file.

```
root@ubuntu: /home/shri/mjproj
obj-m +=parameter.o
all:
        make -C /lib/modules/$(shell uname -r)/build M=$(PWD) modules
clean:
        make -C /lib/modules/$(shell uname -r)/build M=$(PWD) clean
```


Use make command to compile file.

Now use sudo insmod parameter.ko paramTest=2

command to insert the module. Using this command we will pass value 2 to paramTest parameter.

We can see the output using dmesg command.

We can see "Value of paramTest=2" message displayed as output.

```
root@ubuntu:/home/shri/mjproj# vi Makefile
root@ubuntu:/home/shri/mjproj# make
make -C /lib/modules/3.0.0-16-generic/build M=/home/shri/mjproj modules
make[1]: Entering directory `/usr/src/linux-headers-3.0.0-16-generic'
  Building modules, stage 2.
  MODPOST 1 modules
make[1]: Leaving directory `/usr/src/linux-headers-3.0.0-16-generic'
root@ubuntu:/home/shri/mjproj# sudo insmod parameter.ko paramTest=2
root@ubuntu:/home/shri/mjproj# dmesg |tail -5
[  768.380627] Showing the parameter demo
[  768.380637] VALUE OF PARAMTEST IS: 2
root@ubuntu:/home/shri/mjproj#
```

We have completed passing the single parameter. Great!

So now let's check how we can pass multiple parameters at a time.

Parameter Array:

To pass multiple parameters we need to pass parameter array.

Go through below program of passing parameter array.

```c
#include<linux/init.h>
#include<linux/module.h>
#include<linux/moduleparam.h>

MODULE_LICENSE("GPL");

int paramArray[3];
module_param_array(paramArray, int,NULL,
S_IWUSR|S_IRUSR);

static int array_init(void)
{
    printk("Into the parameter Array
demo");
    printk("Array elements are
:%d\t%d\t%d",paramArray[0],paramArray[1],
paramArray[2]);
    return 0;
}

static void array_exit(void)
{
    printk("Exiting the array parameter
demo");
}

module_init(array_init);
module_exit(array_exit);
```

Here we used array of size equals to size of int as 3.

To pass array as a parameter we need to use module_param_array() function instead of module_param() function.

Here along with other parameter it has a counter, which records the number of parameters passed. In our program we have not used this feature, so set its value as 0.

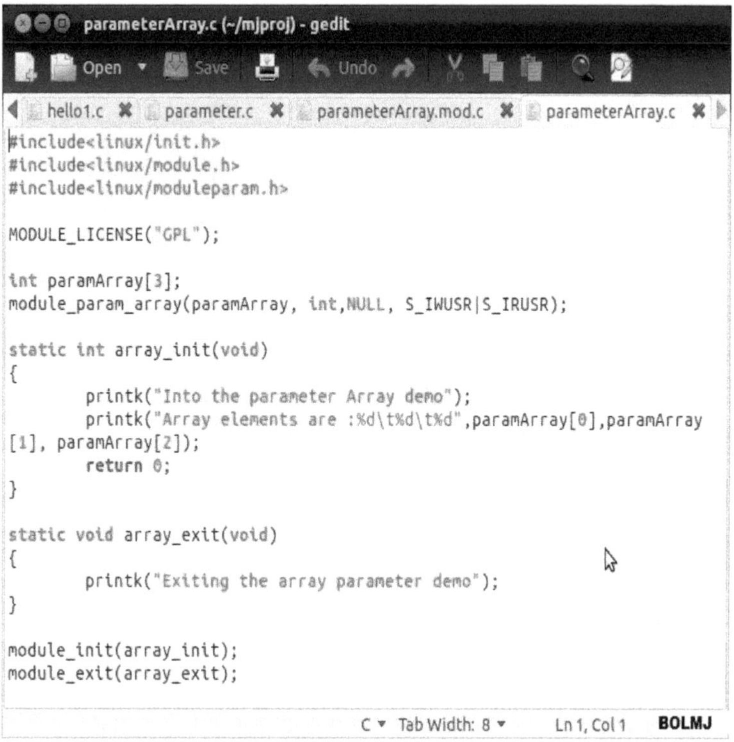

```c
#include<linux/init.h>
#include<linux/module.h>
#include<linux/moduleparam.h>

MODULE_LICENSE("GPL");

int paramArray[3];
module_param_array(paramArray, int,NULL, S_IWUSR|S_IRUSR);

static int array_init(void)
{
        printk("Into the parameter Array demo");
        printk("Array elements are :%d\t%d\t%d",paramArray[0],paramArray
[1], paramArray[2]);
        return 0;
}

static void array_exit(void)
{
        printk("Exiting the array parameter demo");
}

module_init(array_init);
module_exit(array_exit);
```

We pass sudo insmod parameterArray.ko paramArray=1, 2, 3 command along with parameter array to load module.

When we perform dmesg operation then we can see three numbers as output on the screen.

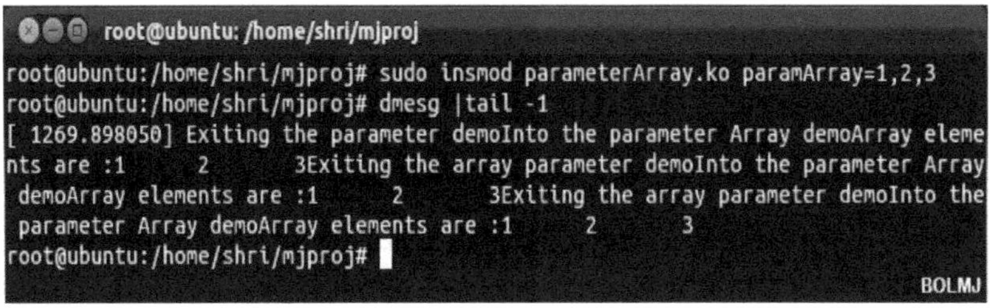

root@ubuntu: /home/shri/mjproj

```
root@ubuntu:/home/shri/mjproj# sudo insmod parameterArray.ko paramArray=1,2,3
root@ubuntu:/home/shri/mjproj# dmesg |tail -1
[ 1269.898050] Exiting the parameter demoInto the parameter Array demoArray eleme
nts are :1        2        3Exiting the array parameter demoInto the parameter Array
 demoArray elements are :1        2        3Exiting the array parameter demoInto the
 parameter Array demoArray elements are :1        2        3
root@ubuntu:/home/shri/mjproj#
```


Yeah, we got array of parameters as an output!

Play more with this program to pass more number of parameters of different types.

Chapter 8
Process Related Program

In our computer many processes are running at same time. Now we will learn a basic program which provides us information about the process running in our system.

Program will provide information about the running process, the process that has stopped and the process id of particular processes and so on.

Whenever we need this data we can utilize this program snippet to get related information.

Program:

```c
#include<linux/init.h>
#include<linux/module.h>
#include<linux/sched.h>

MODULE_LICENSE("GPL");

static int test_init(void)
{
    struct task_struct *task;
    for_each_process(task)
    {
        printk("process Name :%s\t
PID:%d\t Process State:%ld\n",task-
>comm,task->pid, task->state);
    }
    return 0;
}

static void test_exit(void)
{
    printk(KERN_INFO "Clearing up.\n");
}

module_init(test_init);
module_exit(test_exit);
```

In Linux every process is attached with its own
process ID and flag reflecting current status of
that process.

sched.h header file need to include when we write process related program.

We can use pointer of task_struct structure to get further information about the process.

Above written program will provide us process ID and status of process running in our computer.

Here we have created pointer called as task and we have used that pointer to display process related information on output screen.

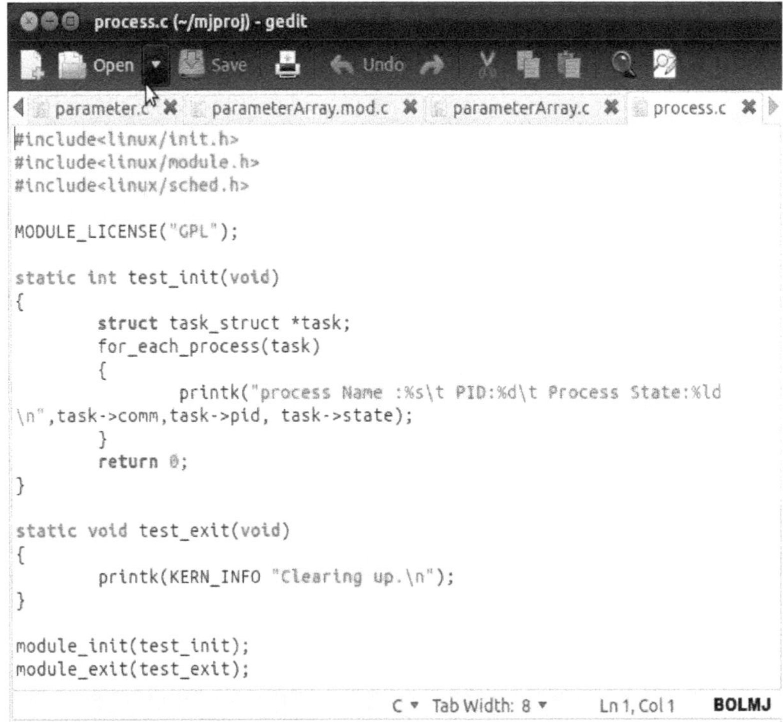


```c
#include<linux/init.h>
#include<linux/module.h>
#include<linux/sched.h>

MODULE_LICENSE("GPL");

static int test_init(void)
{
        struct task_struct *task;
        for_each_process(task)
        {
                printk("process Name :%s\t PID:%d\t Process State:%ld
\n",task->comm,task->pid, task->state);
        }
        return 0;
}

static void test_exit(void)
{
        printk(KERN_INFO "Clearing up.\n");
}

module_init(test_init);
module_exit(test_exit);
```


Once we run this program we can observe list of processes running in our system.

In this way we can get the information of processes running in our system.

```
root@ubuntu:/home/shri/mjproj# sudo rmmod process.ko
root@ubuntu:/home/shri/mjproj# sudo insmod process.ko
root@ubuntu:/home/shri/mjproj# dmesg |tail -20
[ 1762.454556] process Name :applet.py    PID:1791         Process State:1
[ 1762.454562] process Name :bash         PID:1803         Process State:1
[ 1762.454568] process Name :ubuntuone-syncd    PID:1867         Process State:1
[ 1762.454574] process Name :update-notifier    PID:1897         Process State:1
[ 1762.454581] process Name :system-service-    PID:1929         Process State:1
[ 1762.454587] process Name :update-manager     PID:1993         Process State:1
[ 1762.454594] process Name :mount.ntfs PID:2102         Process State:1
[ 1762.454600] process Name :mount.ntfs PID:2109         Process State:1
[ 1762.454606] process Name :libreoffice        PID:2113         Process State:1
[ 1762.454613] process Name :oosplash.bin       PID:2114         Process State:1
[ 1762.454619] process Name :soffice.bin        PID:2129         Process State:1
[ 1762.454625] process Name :deja-dup-monito    PID:2146         Process State:1
[ 1762.454632] process Name :kworker/1:0        PID:2406         Process State:1
[ 1762.454639] process Name :kworker/u:0        PID:2437         Process State:1
[ 1762.454645] process Name :kworker/0:1        PID:2783         Process State:1
[ 1762.454651] process Name :kworker/2:2        PID:2808         Process State:1
[ 1762.454658] process Name :kworker/1:2        PID:2820         Process State:1
[ 1762.454664] process Name :kworker/0:2        PID:2960         Process State:1
[ 1762.454671] process Name :sudo       PID:2970         Process State:1
[ 1762.454676] process Name :insmod     PID:2971         Process State:0
root@ubuntu:/home/shri/mjproj#
```


Search using this process id on internet to get more information about a particular process. From this output we can see the running process , running application and the state of process.

This is just a start! Go ahead with this base line program and try out yourself to add features to provide more process related information by upgrading this program.

Start modifying this program and create innovative stuff right here.

Guys, till now we have learnt parameter passing program, parameter array passing program and process explorer program in the above chapter.

In the next chapter we will learn about character device driver.

Chapter 9
Character Device Driver

We have learnt how to write basic device driver now we will learn about how to write character device driver.

Remember the points which we learnt in the previous chapter of Linux kernel that; In Linux device is also considered as a file. This device file name works as a bridge between application in system and actual device file.

Device number is very important for communication between device file and the device.

Device file number is a pair of two numbers: one is major number and another is minor number. <major, minor>.

In our system many devices can use some common major number but they should contain different minor number associated with them. Kernel uses Minor number to identify the exact device that has been connected to system.

To see all character device drivers present in our system, give following command in terminal window.

```
$ ls -l /dev/ grep "^c"
```

```
root@ubuntu: /home/shri/mjproj
root@ubuntu:/home/shri/mjproj# ls -l /dev/ |grep "crw"
crw-rw----  1 root video    10, 175 2013-04-06 10:10 agpgart
crw-------  1 root root     10, 235 2013-04-06 10:10 autofs
crw-------  1 root root     10, 234 2013-04-06 10:10 btrfs-control
crw-------  1 root root      5,   1 2013-04-06 10:10 console
crw-------  1 root root     10,  60 2013-04-06 10:10 cpu_dma_latency
crw-------  1 root root     10,  61 2013-04-06 10:10 ecryptfs
crw-rw----  1 root video    29,   0 2013-04-06 10:10 fb0
crw-rw----  1 root video    29,   1 2013-04-06 10:10 fb1
crw-rw-rw-  1 root root      1,   7 2013-04-06 10:10 full
crw-rw-rw-  1 root fuse     10, 229 2013-04-06 10:10 fuse
crw-------  1 root root     10, 228 2013-04-06 10:10 hpet
crw-------  1 root root      1,  11 2013-04-06 10:10 kmsg
crw-------  1 root root     10, 227 2013-04-06 10:10 mcelog
crw-------  1 root root    251,   1 2013-04-06 10:10 mei
crw-r-----  1 root kmem      1,   1 2013-04-06 10:10 mem
crw-------  1 root root     10,  59 2013-04-06 10:10 network_latency
crw-------  1 root root     10,  58 2013-04-06 10:10 network_throughput
crw-rw-rw-  1 root root      1,   3 2013-04-06 10:10 null
crw-------  1 root root      1,  12 2013-04-06 10:10 oldmem
crw-r-----  1 root kmem      1,   4 2013-04-06 10:10 port
crw-------  1 root root    108,   0 2013-04-06 10:10 ppp
crw-------  1 root root     10,   1 2013-04-06 10:10 psaux
crw-rw-rw-  1 root tty       5,   2 2013-04-06 10:43 ptmx
crw-rw-rw-  1 root root      1,   8 2013-04-06 10:10 random
crw-rw-r--+ 1 root root     10,  62 2013-04-06 10:10 rfkill
crw-------  1 root root    254,   0 2013-04-06 10:10 rtc0
crw-rw----  1 root disk     21,   0 2013-04-06 10:10 sg0
```

ls -l /dev: Command shows all drivers present in our system.

Output of this command will display as given below:

```
root@ubuntu: /home/shri/mjproj
drwxr-xr-x  2 root root             60 2013-04-06 10:10 cpu
crw-------  1 root root        10,  60 2013-04-06 10:10 cpu_dma_latency
drwxr-xr-x  6 root root            120 2013-04-06 15:39 disk
drwxr-xr-x  2 root root            120 2013-04-06 10:10 dri
lrwxrwxrwx  1 root root              3 2013-04-06 10:10 dvd -> sr0
lrwxrwxrwx  1 root root              3 2013-04-06 10:10 dvdrw -> sr0
crw-------  1 root root        10,  61 2013-04-06 10:10 ecryptfs
crw-rw----  1 root video       29,   0 2013-04-06 10:10 fb0
crw-rw----  1 root video       29,   1 2013-04-06 10:10 fb1
lrwxrwxrwx  1 root root             13 2013-04-06 10:10 fd -> /proc/self/fd
crw-rw-rw-  1 root root         1,   7 2013-04-06 10:10 full
crw-rw-rw-  1 root fuse       10, 229 2013-04-06 10:10 fuse
crw-------  1 root root       10, 228 2013-04-06 10:10 hpet
drwxr-xr-x  4 root root            380 2013-04-06 10:10 input
crw-------  1 root root         1,  11 2013-04-06 10:10 kmsg
srw-rw-rw-  1 root root              0 2013-04-06 10:10 log
brw-rw----  1 root disk        7,   0 2013-04-06 10:10 loop0
brw-rw----  1 root disk        7,   1 2013-04-06 10:10 loop1
brw-rw----  1 root disk        7,   2 2013-04-06 10:10 loop2
brw-rw----  1 root disk        7,   3 2013-04-06 10:10 loop3
brw-rw----  1 root disk        7,   4 2013-04-06 10:10 loop4
brw-rw----  1 root disk        7,   5 2013-04-06 10:10 loop5
brw-rw----  1 root disk        7,   6 2013-04-06 10:10 loop6
brw-rw----  1 root disk        7,   7 2013-04-06 10:10 loop7
drwxr-xr-x  2 root root             60 2013-04-06 15:39 mapper
crw-------  1 root root       10, 227 2013-04-06 10:10 mcelog
crw-------  1 root root      251,   1 2013-04-06 10:10 mei
crw-r-----  1 root kmem        1,   1 2013-04-06 10:10 mem
```

In above image brw: represents Block device driver and crw represents character device driver.

Major and minor numbers are stored in dev_t variable.

[12 bit Major + 20 bit Minor =32 Bit dev_t]

MKDEV(int major, int minor) command use to create device dev variable.

To connect device file to device driver we need to perform following two steps:

1. Register our device by giving <major, minor> number of device.
2. Connect device file operations and device driver functions to each other.

To get device number following API form <linux/fs.h> are very important.

```
1. int register_chardev_region(dev_t
   first,unsigned int count, char *name);
2. int alloc_chardev_region(dev_t
   *dev,unsigned int firstminor,unsigned
   int count,char *name);
3. void unregister_chardev_region(dev_t
   first,unsigned int count);
```

- Fiirst API registers a device equivalent to cnt count number.

- If this function works without any error then it return zero. If it faces any problem then it returns negative number.

- Second API automatically finds out free Major Number and register it .In general first minor number is '0' number.

- Third API is used to free our device number; once we have done with that device number. This API is useful in clean-up functions.

[REF:Linux Device Driver Book]

Program to show device number:

```c
#include <linux/module.h>
#include <linux/version.h>
#include <linux/kernel.h>
#include <linux/init.h>
#include <linux/fs.h>

static dev_t first;   //globle variable for
the device no

int __init ofd_init(void) /*const*/
{
        printk(KERN_INFO "NAMSAKAR:ofd
reg");
      if (alloc_chrdev_region(&first, 0, 3,
"Mahesh") <0)
      {
            return -1;
      }
      printk(KERN_INFO "<Major,Minor>: <%d
,%d> \n", MAJOR(first),MINOR(first));
        return 0;
}

static void __exit
ofd_exit(void)/*Destructor*/
{
        unregister_chrdev_region(first, 3);
      printk(KERN_INFO "by Gn:ofd unreg");
}

module_init(ofd_init);
module_exit(ofd_exit);

MODULE_LICENSE("GPL");
MODULE_DESCRIPTION("OUR FIRST character
DRIVER");
```

After running this program we can see that Device named as "Mahesh" has been created along with his own major and minor number.

```
root@ubuntu: /home/shri/mjproj/mjlearn
root@ubuntu:/home/shri/mjproj/mjlearn# vi Makefile
root@ubuntu:/home/shri/mjproj/mjlearn# make
make -C /lib/modules/3.0.0-16-generic/build M=/home/shri/mjproj/mjlearn modules
make[1]: Entering directory `/usr/src/linux-headers-3.0.0-16-generic'
  CC [M]  /home/shri/mjproj/mjlearn/mjlearnchar.o
  Building modules, stage 2.
  MODPOST 1 modules
  CC      /home/shri/mjproj/mjlearn/mjlearnchar.mod.o
  LD [M]  /home/shri/mjproj/mjlearn/mjlearnchar.ko
make[1]: Leaving directory `/usr/src/linux-headers-3.0.0-16-generic'
root@ubuntu:/home/shri/mjproj/mjlearn# sudo insmod mjlearnchar.ko
root@ubuntu:/home/shri/mjproj/mjlearn# sudo rmmod mjlearnchar.ko
root@ubuntu:/home/shri/mjproj/milearn# dmesg |tail -10
[ 2984.749776] NAMSAKAR:ofd reg
[ 2984.749780] <Major,Minor>: <250 ,0>
[ 2993.235961] by Gn:ofd unreg
root@ubuntu:/home/shri/mjproj/mjlearn#
```

Above output window shows major and minor number of device. We have shown this output on screen using printk function.

```
🗙🗕🔲   root@ubuntu: /home/shri/mjproj/mjlearn
root@ubuntu:/home/shri/mjproj/mjlearn# sudo insmod mjlearnchar.ko
root@ubuntu:/home/shri/mjproj/mjlearn# cat /proc/devices |head -28 |tail -10
116 alsa
128 ptm
136 pts
180 usb
189 usb_device
216 rfcomm
226 drm
250 Mahesh
251 mei
252 usbmon
root@ubuntu:/home/shri/mjproj/mjlearn# ls -l /dev |grep "250"
root@ubuntu:/home/shri/mjproj/mjlearn# sudo mknod /dev/mjcd1 c 250 1
root@ubuntu:/home/shri/mjproj/mjlearn# sudo mknod /dev/mjcd2 c 250 2
root@ubuntu:/home/shri/mjproj/mjlearn# ls -l /dev/mjcd*
crw-r--r-- 1 root root 250, 1 2013-04-06 11:07 /dev/mjcd1
crw-r--r-- 1 root root 250, 2 2013-04-06 11:07 /dev/mjcd2
root@ubuntu:/home/shri/mjproj/mjlearn#
```

Above screenshot shows that we go to /proc/device to check if our device is really got created there or not. We can observe that the device called 'mahesh' has been created.

Then we go to /dev to see if the device file is generated or not. Then we have created a node using mknod command. There we can see file has been created for our device. We can perform this task automatically also. We will learn same thing in next chapter.

So stay tuned...

Chapter 10
Character Device Driver: File Operations.

Character device driver is connected to file and performs all the tasks with the help of file. We can declare all file related functions and then we can open, read write, close that file as per our need.

Now we will go through each function and print name of that function in the program below.

Basic character device driver file operation program will look as under:

```c
#include <linux/module.h>
#include <linux/version.h>
#include <linux/kernel.h>
#include <linux/init.h>
#include <linux/fs.h>
#include <linux/device.h>
#include <linux/cdev.h>

static dev_t first;  //globle variable
for the device no
static struct cdev c_dev; //globle var
for char struct
static struct class *cl; //globle var
for device class

static int my_open(struct inode *i,
struct file *f)
{
    printk(KERN_INFO "Driver
:open()\n");
    return 0;
}
static int my_close(struct inode *i ,
struct file *f)
{
    printk(KERN_INFO
"Driver:close()\n");
    return 0;
}
static ssize_t my_read(struct file
*f,char __user *buf,size_t len,loff_t
*off)
{
    printk(KERN_INFO
"Driver:read()\n");
    return 0;
}
```

```c
static int my_write(struct file *f,const
char __user *buf,size_t len,loff_t *off)
{
    printk(KERN_INFO "Driver:write()\n");
    return len;
}

static struct file_operations pugs_fops=
{
    .owner = THIS_MODULE,
    .open = my_open,
    .release =my_close,
    .read =my_read,
    .write =my_write
};

static int __init ofcd_init(void)
/*const*/
{
        printk(KERN_INFO "NAMSAKAR:ofd
reg");
    if (alloc_chrdev_region(&first, 0, 3,
"Mahesh") < 0)
    {
        return -1;
    }
    if ((cl = class_create(THIS_MODULE,
"chardrv")) == NULL)
    {
        unregister_chrdev_region(first,
1);
        return -1;
    }
```

```c
if (device_create(cl, NULL ,first, NULL,
"mynull") == NULL)
        {
                class_destroy(cl);
                unregister_chrdev_region(first,
1);
                return -1;
        }
        cdev_init(&c_dev, &pugs_fops);
        if (cdev_add(&c_dev, first, 1)== -1)
        {
                device_destroy(cl,first);
                class_destroy(cl);

        unregister_chrdev_region(first,1);
                return -1;
        }
        return 0;
}

static void __exit
ofcd_exit(void)/*Destructor*/
{
        cdev_del(&c_dev);
        device_destroy(cl, first);
        class_destroy(cl);

unregister_chrdev_region(first,1);
        printk(KERN_INFO "by Gn:ofd unreg");
}


module_init(ofcd_init);
module_exit(ofcd_exit);

MODULE_LICENSE("GPL");
MODULE_AUTHOR("MJ");
MODULE_DESCRIPTION("OUR FIRST character
DRIVER:automatic");
```

When to include which .h header file?

- #include <Linux/init.h>: Basic Initialization.

- #include <linux/module.h>: Writing any modules.

- #include <linux/version.h>: To get linux version related data.

- #include <linux/kernel.h>: Allowed to use printk() function.

- #include <linux/fs.h>: To perform file related operations.

- #include <linux/device.h>: To perform device related operations.

- #include <linux/cdev.h>: To create a character device driver with major and minor number.

- #include <linux/slab.h> :Allow to use kmalloc() function.

- #include <linux/errno.h>: File contains error codes.

- #include <linux/types.h>: To get support to use data types like size_t ,dev_t .

- #include <linux/fcntl.h>: For o_accmode .

- #include <asm/system.h>: To use cli(), _flags .

- #include <asm/uaccess.h>: To use functions like copy_from /to _users.

Functions provided in module.h file:

MODULE_ALIAS(_alias)	To provide module name and information in user space.
MODULE_LICENSE(_license)	Name of license of the modules to be used.
MODULE_AUTHOR()	Writer of module.
MODULE_DESCRIPTION()	Provide working details of module.
MODULE_PARAM()	Parameter which pass while loading of the module.
MODULE_VERSION()	Version of module under use.

When we give modinfo module name .ko command then all the module related information in terminal window is obtained

Points to note regarding file operations:

In above code open and close functions returns integer value; when functions returns value as zero '0". It means function executed successfully. If functions return some negative numbers then there must be some problem while executing these functions.

Read and write functions returns some positive numbers this numbers shows that how much data bites are write or read. That's why return type of these functions are always ssize_t.

There is one interesting thing I want to tell you!! read() function writes len bytes amount of data in buf buffer and returns bytes count as a return value. It means read function actually writes data in user space buffer so that user can read that data and use for further task.

Isn't it strange news that read function writes in buffer.☺

Important code snippets:

```
loff_t (*llseek) (struct file *, loff_t, int);
```

Here llseek method changes current read write position of file, loff_t means log offset.Gives number of shift in position.

```
ssize_t (*read) (struct file *, char __user *, size_t, loff_t *);
```

This function uses while taking data from driver. If there is no data available then it gives EINVAL (invalid argument) as error message.

```
int (*open) (struct inode *, struct file *);
```

To opening device is the first thing performed on device file.

struct module *owner

This pointer points to our module and prevents to remove the application when module is running and user tries to remove it.

Generally his name remains as THIS_MODULE and his definition is located in <linux/module.h> header file.

Open Method:

Open method works as below:

- ✓ Check if the device is ready and is there any related error.
- ✓ If the device is opening for first time then initialize that device.
- ✓ Update f_op pointer.
- ✓ Reserve the space for file->private_data structure and keep the data in allocated space.

Release Method:

Release method works as below:

- ✓ Release the space allocated by open method in file->private_data.

- ✓ Close the device.

Read and write method:

- ✓ ssize_t read(struct file *filp, char __user *buff, size_t count, loff_t *offp);
- ✓ ssize_t write(struct file *filp, const char __user *buff,size_t count, loff_t *offp);
- ✓ Here flip is a file pointer.

- ✓ count means size of data to be transferred.

- ✓ buff means user buffer in which data will be stored while performing read and write operation.

- ✓ offp [log offset type pointer] Shows the position of file which user is using.

- ✓ Return value ssize_t means signed size type.

Go through the below diagram to see how above method works.

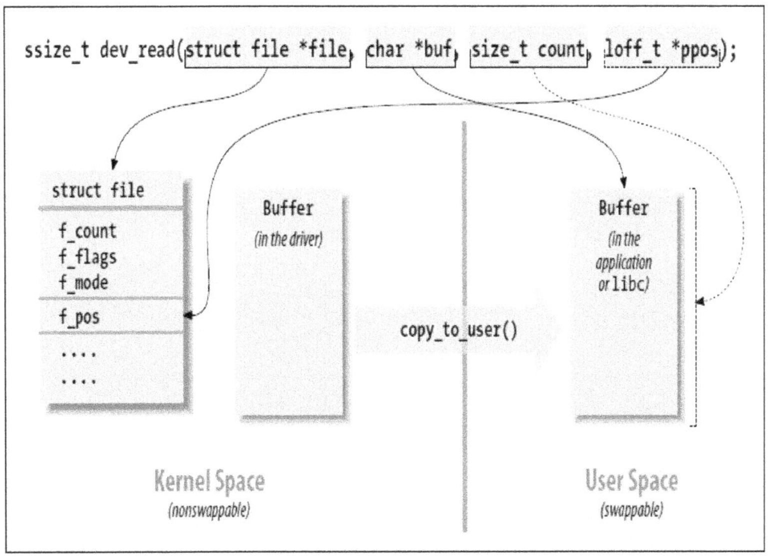

[Ref:Linux Device Driver Book]

Rules for read and write method:

If return number is equal to count number then that number of bytes gets transfered.

If retun number is possitive and lower than count then that data will be transferred.

If retun number is zero then it means file has finished.

Negative return value represents error number.

<linux/errno.h> file conatins details about that error number.

It contains -EINTR [interrupt system call],

-EFAULT [bad address] like error messages.

Summary of device driver file operations:

Process	User Functions	Kernel Functions
Load the module.	insmod	module_init()
Open device	fopen	file_operations:open
Read from device	fread	file_operations:read
write in device	fwrite	file_operations:write
Close the device	fclose	file_operations:release
Remove module.	rmmod	module_exit()

[Ref:FreeSoftwareMagazine]

Chapter 11
PCI Device Driver

<u>PCI means Peripheral Component interconnect.</u>

In computer PCI bus is used to connect peripheral devices like graphics card and lan card to our computer. This bus is connected to CPU processor via south bridge and then North Bridge.

In this way when we watch video on our desktop or send data to server using internet we indirectly use PCI bus only.

PCI bus has very good data transfer rate. Data transfer rate of PCIe is 250 MB per lane up to maximum of 8 GB.

PCI has multiple types namely PCI, PCI Express, PCI Extender and Mini PCI.

Clock rate of PCI devices is from 25 Hz to 33 Hz.

PCI slot on motherboard.

In this chapter we will learn about the working of PCI device driver and their features.

PCI devices are identified by their vendor ID, Device ID and Class code.

Use following command to see PCI devices present in our system.

lspci

After executing this command in terminal window you can observe some numbers in front of each device name.

First number is PCI bus number then PCI device number and the last one indicates device function.

```
root@ubuntu: /home/shri/mjproj/mjlearn
root@ubuntu:/home/shri/mjproj/mjlearn# lspci
00:00.0 Host bridge: Intel Corporation 2nd Generation Core Processor Family DRAM
 Controller (rev 09)
00:01.0 PCI bridge: Intel Corporation Xeon E3-1200/2nd Generation Core Processor
 Family PCI Express Root Port (rev 09)
00:02.0 VGA compatible controller: Intel Corporation 2nd Generation Core Process
or Family Integrated Graphics Controller (rev 09)
00:16.0 Communication controller: Intel Corporation 6 Series/C200 Series Chipset
 Family MEI Controller #1 (rev 04)
00:1a.0 USB Controller: Intel Corporation 6 Series/C200 Series Chipset Family US
B Enhanced Host Controller #2 (rev 05)
00:1b.0 Audio device: Intel Corporation 6 Series/C200 Series Chipset Family High
 Definition Audio Controller (rev 05)
00:1c.0 PCI bridge: Intel Corporation 6 Series/C200 Series Chipset Family PCI Ex
press Root Port 1 (rev b5)
00:1c.1 PCI bridge: Intel Corporation 6 Series/C200 Series Chipset Family PCI Ex
press Root Port 2 (rev b5)
00:1c.3 PCI bridge: Intel Corporation 6 Series/C200 Series Chipset Family PCI Ex
press Root Port 4 (rev b5)
00:1c.4 PCI bridge: Intel Corporation 6 Series/C200 Series Chipset Family PCI Ex
press Root Port 5 (rev b5)
00:1c.5 PCI bridge: Intel Corporation 6 Series/C200 Series Chipset Family PCI Ex
press Root Port 6 (rev b5)
00:1d.0 USB Controller: Intel Corporation 6 Series/C200 Series Chipset Family US
B Enhanced Host Controller #1 (rev 05)
00:1f.0 ISA bridge: Intel Corporation HM67 Express Chipset Family LPC Controller
 (rev 05)
00:1f.2 SATA controller: Intel Corporation 6 Series/C200 Series Chipset Family 6
 port SATA AHCI Controller (rev 05)
00:1f.3 SMBus: Intel Corporation 6 Series/C200 Series Chipset Family SMBus Contr
oller (rev 05)
```

To see all PCI devices in tree structure format use the command given below.

lspci -t

PCI device driver does not require probing. In this driver pci_dev data structure gets utilized.

PCI devices have three address regions:

1) Configuration Space
2) Input Output Port
3) Device Memory.

Configuration space can work on only one slot at a time.

Input output port; Device Memory location shares all the devices in single PCI bus.

Special functions in kernel works on registers in configuration space.

Every PCI slot contains 4 interrupt pins. Only one pin can be used at a time by CPU.

During system boot, firmware of PCI device performs Hardware initialization and every region gets connected to different address.

To which address Current region gets connected can be read from configuration space. That's why PCI device driver does not require explicit probing.

[Note :USB device driver requires probing to use device.]

After turning on PCI device hardware doesn't start completely; it only response for functions related to configuration. Firmware reads and delivers register data from PCI controller to configuration address.

While booting, Firmware allocates address region to PCI devices at the same time device driver sees connection between memory region of device and IO region.

Configuration Registers of PCI are as given below:

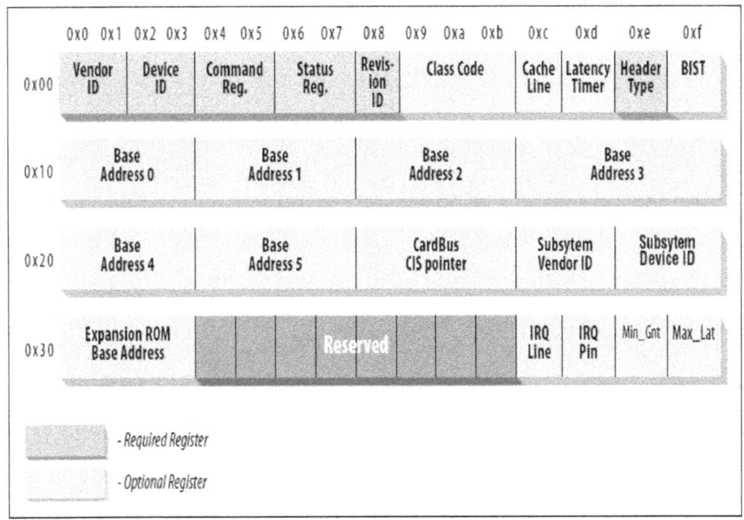

[REF:Essential linux Device Driver-Alan Cox-Pearson]

Input output region contains registers and memory region contains data.

Video card: Here in input output space, control register and memory region gets connected to frame buffer.

Direct Memory Access [DMA]

Process of connecting system memory to device without CPU interference is called as Direct Memory access.

Without using processor we can move data in memory. DMA controller in south bridge of PCI bus can also take control of BUS and perform direct memory transfer.

DMA Buffer:

Inorder to send data in system to LCD screen, user needs to write pixel data in frame buffer then LCD controller connects with it in timely basis and shows the fresh data on the screen. This memory space in the system is called as DMA buffer.

Module Device Table:

By providing pci_device_id data structure to user we can provide Hot Plug feature. Also module loader get to know about which module works for hardware.

MODULE_DEVICE_TABLE (pci, i810_ids)

Above function create local variable and point it to pci_device_id data structure. Related modules will be searched and put in to modules.pcimap.

When new device gets hot plugged then hot plug system uses modules pcimap to load matching driver.

Basic PCI device Driver:

First of all we need to create device:

```
Code for Basic Device Driver:
#include <linux/pci.h>
//Functions required for us will be taken
from PCI .h file.

#define MY_VENDOR_ID 0xABCD
#define MY_DEVICE_ID_NET 0xEF01
//Record the supported device.

//First we will create a device.

struct pci_device_id
network_driver_pci_table[] __devinitdata
=
{
  {
    { MY_VENDOR_ID, /* Interface chip
manufacturer ID */
      MY_DEVICE_ID_NET, /* Device ID for
the network */
      PCI_ANY_ID, /* Subvendor ID wild
card */
      PCI_ANY_ID, /* Subdevice ID wild
card */
      0, 0, /* class and classmask are
unspecified */
      network_driver_private_data
    }, {0},
};

//In above code we are given PCI driver
related data.
```

```c
struct pci_driver network_pci_driver =
{
    .name = "ntwrk", /* Unique name */
    .probe = net_driver_probe,
    .remove =
__devexit_p(net_driver_remove),
    .id_table =
network_driver_pci_table,
    /* suspend() and resume()  optional
methods*/
};

// Here basic functions of our device
driver gets declared.
Which includes function related to
connecting device driver name, removing
device driver. Also it contains device
ID table.

static int __init
network_driver_init(void)
{
    pci_register_driver(&network_pci_dr
iver);
    return 0;
}

// Here device driver gets initialize.
```

```
Static void __exit
network_driver_exit(void)

{

    pci_unregister_driver(&network_pci_dr
iver);
}
// Here we define unregister function
which will be get called after removing
driver.


module_init(network_driver_init);
module_exit(network_driver_exit);
MODULE_DEVICE_TABLE(pci,
network_driver_pci_table);
```

Probing function performs following task:

- Enable PCI device.

- Find information of resource: Input output
  bus address, Interrupt request.

- Assign driver related data structure.

- Perform self-Registration.

Important code snippets of PCI device driver:

`#include <linux/pci.h>`	This header supports for PCI related registers and IDs
`struct pci_dev;`	This structure shows PCI device in kernel.
`struct pci_driver;`	This structure indicates PCI device driver.
`struct pci_device_id;`	Give information about supported PCI devices.
`int pci_register_driver(struct pci_driver *drv);`	Register PCI device to PCI core.
`int pci_module_init(struct`	Initiate modules.

pci_driver *drv);	
void pci_unregister_driver(struct pci_driver *drv);	Unload driver and remove PCI devices connected to driver.
int pci_enable_device(stru ct pci_dev *dev);	This function gets used in probe function. Start device assign interrupt, input, output region.
int pci_read_config_byte(s truct pci_dev *dev, int where, u8 *val);	This function used to work on configuration sapce.In this function pci_bus uses function related to bus.
int pci_read_config_word(s truct pci_dev *dev, int where, u16 *val);	
int pci_read_config_dword(	Meaning of words in

`struct pci_dev *dev, int where, u32 *val);`	function: 8 bit data transfer = byte
`int pci_write_config_byte (struct pci_dev *dev, int where, u8 *val);`	16 bit data transfer = word
`int pci_write_config_word (struct pci_dev *dev, int where, u16 *val);`	32 bit data transfer = dword To read from PCI configuration space= read
`int pci_write_config_dword (struct pci_dev *dev, int where, u32 *val);`	To write in PCI configuration space= write Starting offset of configuration space = where To return error code number= val PCI device pointer = dev

pci_resource_start()	This function
pci_resource_len()	works on Input
pci_resource_end()	and output
pci_resource_flags()	regions.
	Following
	functions get
	information
	regarding base
	address, length,
	last
	address, control
	flag
	respectively.

After reading this chapter we understand about 'How to write basic PCI device driver?'

You can find detailed PCI code which runs in our operation system from the location given below:

drivers/net/, drivers/scsi/, drivers/video/

In Linux system go to Documentation/pci.txt location to find more about PCI device driver.

PCI interface is connected to mother board. This interface is useful while writing device driver for Graphics card and Network card.

Let's learn USB device driver in next chapter.

Chapter 12
USB Device Driver Fundamentals

We connect pen drive, mouse, keyboard, headphone to our computer using USB port. Using this port we communicate with processor inside system.They all uses USB bus (Universal Serial Bus) to transfer data using serial method.

In last chapter we learnt about some very useful information regarding Character driver and PCI device driver. In this chapter we will learn more interesting...Live Device Driver...!!

Architecture of USB device driver:

USB host controller works as a Master and Ask each USB device if anyone have some data to send. USB Device does not allow performing data transfer without asking host controller. System has USB host controller driver to host USB and USB devices has USB client driver in it.

USB core provides routine and structure required for both drivers.USB core is the main part of USB driver system.

Kernel has helper thread called as khubd. This thread looks at all ports and checks whether any change happened on any port.

To access USB devices from user space USB file system usbfs is used.

User can take information about USB devices from /dev ,/sys.

Following diagram gives all the detailed information about USB data exchange.

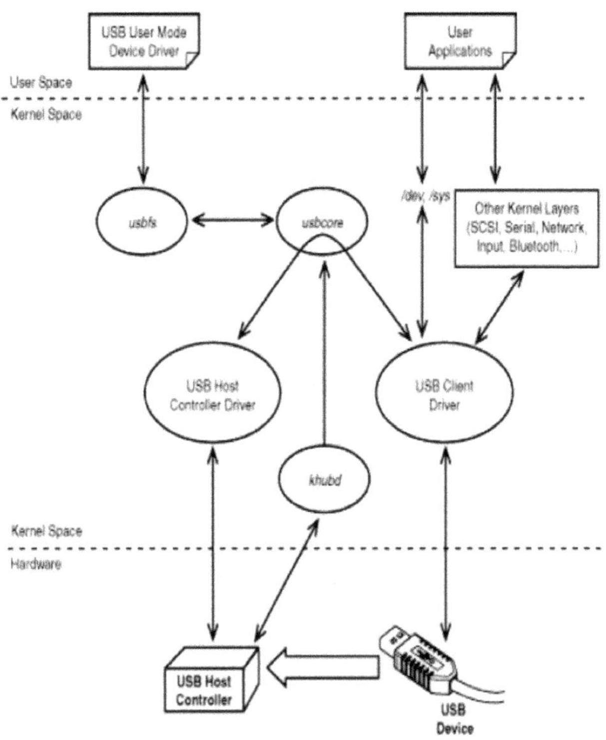

Features of USB bus: To send audio or video data, device can request for fix bandwidth. USB protocol contains some common generic devices which do not require any explicit device driver to install. For example: keyboard, mouse, network devices.

For some special devices we need to write special device driver.

Linux system supports two types of USB drivers:

One which is in the system [USB Device Driver]

Another is in the device [USB gadget driver]

Now let's look in to practical of USB device driver.

For experiment take one USB pen drive and connect it to the computer.

To check that the device has been detected by system, we will give lsusb command in terminal. You can see entry of your pen drive in terminal window. You can also see in below image that my SanDisk pen driver gets detected.

```
root@ubuntu: /home/shri/mjproj/mjlearn
root@ubuntu:/home/shri/mjproj/mjlearn# lsusb
Bus 001 Device 001: ID 1d6b:0002 Linux Foundation 2.0 root hub
Bus 002 Device 001: ID 1d6b:0002 Linux Foundation 2.0 root hub
Bus 003 Device 001: ID 1d6b:0002 Linux Foundation 2.0 root hub
Bus 004 Device 001: ID 1d6b:0003 Linux Foundation 3.0 root hub
Bus 001 Device 002: ID 8087:0024 Intel Corp. Integrated Rate Matching Hub
Bus 002 Device 002: ID 8087:0024 Intel Corp. Integrated Rate Matching Hub
Bus 001 Device 003: ID 0408:2fb1 Quanta Computer, Inc.
Bus 002 Device 015: ID 0781:5567 SanDisk Corp. Cruzer Blade
root@ubuntu:/home/shri/mjproj/mjlearn#
```

Give lsusb –v command To get all the information about pen drive. The information received include the name of vender, vender ID of pen drive and product ID of pen drive. The vender id and product id of my pen driver is 0x0781, 0x5567. We will use this number to write device driver.

[Note: After executing lsusb -v command you will get the information about USB device. It contains some initials which provide some important information.

D= Devices, C= configuration, I= Interface. E= endpoint. We can see more details about this in upcoming chapters]

```
root@ubuntu: /home/shri/mjproj/mjlearn

Bus 002 Device 042: ID 0781:5567 SanDisk Corp. Cruzer Blade
Device Descriptor:
  bLength                 18
  bDescriptorType          1
  bcdUSB                2.00
  bDeviceClass             0 (Defined at Interface level)
  bDeviceSubClass          0
  bDeviceProtocol          0
  bMaxPacketSize0         64
  idVendor            0x0781 SanDisk Corp.
  idProduct           0x5567 Cruzer Blade
  bcdDevice             1.03
  iManufacturer            1 SanDisk
  iProduct                 2 Cruzer Blade
  iSerial                  3 20043411220F42F03487
  bNumConfigurations       1
  Configuration Descriptor:
    bLength                9
    bDescriptorType        2
    wTotalLength          32
    bNumInterfaces         1
    bConfigurationValue    1
    iConfiguration         0
    bmAttributes        0x80
      (Bus Powered)
    MaxPower            200mA
    Interface Descriptor:
      bLength              9
      bDescriptorType      4
      bInterfaceNumber     0
      bAlternateSetting    0
      bNumEndpoints        2
      bInterfaceClass      8 Mass Storage
      bInterfaceSubClass   6 SCSI
      bInterfaceProtocol  80 Bulk (Zip)
      iInterface           0
      Endpoint Descriptor:
        bLength            7
```

[Note :We will learn about latest USB 3.0 in

upcomming chapters.]

USB Device Driver program:

Now we will learn how to write First Basic USB driver program.

```c
#include <linux/module.h>
#include <linux/kernel.h>
#include <linux/usb.h>

static int pen_probe(struct
usb_interface *interface, const struct
usb_device_id *id)
{
    printk (KERN_INFO "Pen
drive(%04X:%04X) plugged\n", id-
>idVendor, id->idProduct);
    return 0;
}

static void pen_disconnect(struct
usb_interface *interface)
{
    printk(KERN_INFO "PEN drive removed
\n");
}

static struct usb_device_id pen_table[]=
{

    { USB_DEVICE(0x0781,0x5567)},
    {}
};
MODULE_DEVICE_TABLE (usb, pen_table);
```

```c
static struct usb_driver pen_driver =
{
        .name = "pen_driver",
        .id_table = pen_table,
        .probe = pen_probe,
        .disconnect = pen_disconnect,
};

static int __init pen_init(void)
{
        return usb_register(&pen_driver);
}
static void __exit pen_exit(void)
{
        usb_deregister(&pen_driver);
}
module_init(pen_init);
module_exit(pen_exit);

MODULE_LICENSE("GPL");
MODULE_AUTHOR ("MJ");
MODULE_DESCRIPTION("USB PEN
REGISTRATION DRIVER");
```

Structure of USB device driver is similar to character device driver. Here we will not register and unregister devices from file and will be using hardware. USB API usb_register and usb_deregister is utilized for the same.

Along with the probe and disconnect, we can use suspend and resume functions as per our requirements. By using these we don't want to use device. In this case, it will go in to suspended mode and will return back in resume mode when we need it.

We can create Device Table to detect devices automatically. We have passed device ID so that once we connect the device driver, it will automatically get started.

For USB device we have to pass first parameter as usb in device table. Then we have to pass name of device ID table.

As soon as we plug, the device probe function runs and on removing the device disconnect function runs.

To run this program we need to create a Makefile for this program. Compile this Makefile using make command to generate .ko file.

Load the module using lsmod command.

Remember one point before loading the module; we need to remove the USB module which is already present in our system [usb-storage]. For this use rmmod usb-storage command so that already existing USB related module will get removed.

Now connect pen drive to system and run dmesg command.

Then remove the USB pen drive and again run dmesg command.

```
root@ubuntu: /home/shri/mjproj/mjlearn
root@ubuntu:/home/shri/mjproj/mjlearn# sudo insmod pen_register.ko
root@ubuntu:/home/shri/mjproj/mjlearn# dmesg | grep MJ
[ 9685.376521] usbcore: registered new interface driver MJ pen_driver
[ 9715.133082] usbcore: deregistering interface driver MJ pen_driver
[ 9732.576190] usbcore: registered new interface driver MJ pen_driver
[ 9737.646870] MJ Pen drive(0781:5567) plugged
[ 9740.045730] MJ PEN drive removed
[ 9740.337460] MJ Pen drive(0781:5567) plugged
[ 9746.954141] MJ PEN drive removed
[ 9771.165196] usbcore: deregistering interface driver MJ pen_driver
[ 9780.545237] usbcore: registered new interface driver MJ pen_driver
[ 9786.489870] MJ Pen drive(0781:5567) plugged
[ 9852.541345] usbcore: deregistering interface driver MJ pen_driver
[ 9852.541379] MJ PEN drive removed
[ 9865.601998] usbcore: registered new interface driver MJ pen_driver
[ 9978.007980] usbcore: deregistering interface driver MJ pen_driver
[10000.338915] usbcore: registered new interface driver MJ pen_driver
root@ubuntu:/home/shri/mjproj/mjlearn#
```

Above screenshot shows that our probe and disconnect function run after plugging and unplugging the device.

Output of function is shown on the screen. That's like a real woking device driver which provides output after external plug and unplug events...Great. Are you enjoying this stuff?...Having fun...yeah!!

It is now time to move further...

Chapter 13
Structure of USB Device Driver

We will learn more about USB internals and structure of USB in detail.

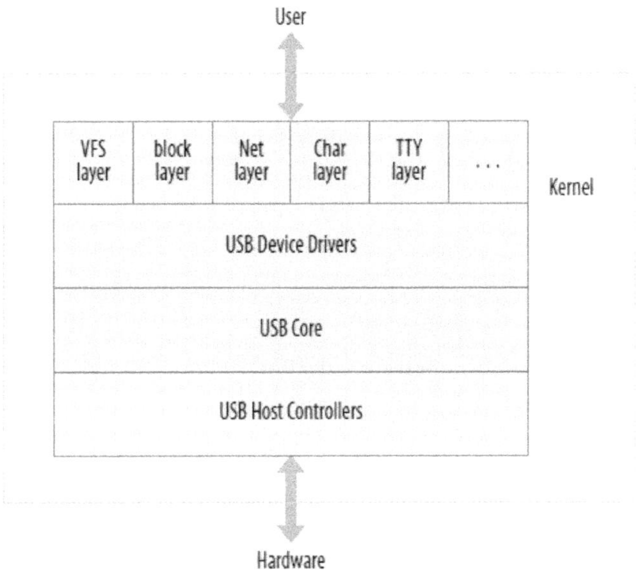

Above image shows that USB driver is exactly between kernel system and hardware.

USB core gets utilized to provide hardware access to USB driver.

Visit the link: www.usb.org to get more information about USB structure

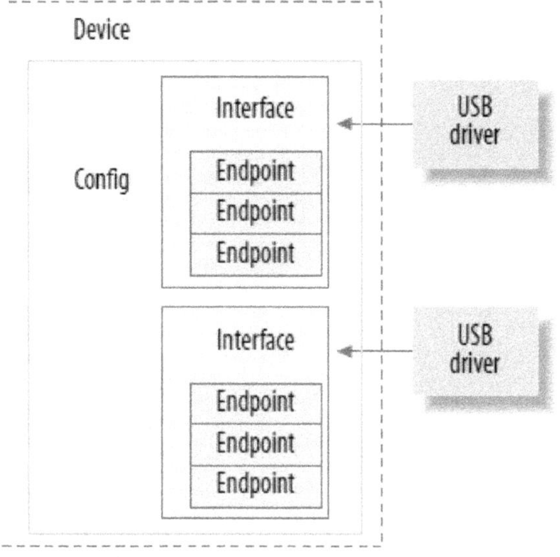

USB devices gets connected to USB driver using USB Interface.

USB endpoints are useful to transfer data inside [IN endpoint] or outside [out endpoint].

The data is transferred in one direction only with the help of data pipe.

Four parts of USB end points:

Control: It is used to configure device, to get information about device and to check status of device by passing commands.

Generally in many devices endpoint 0 perform this operation. This is one and the only endpoint which is bidirectional.

Interrupt: This Endpoint is used to transfer fewer amount of data after some gap of duration. Devices like mouse, keyboard gets controlled by this endpoint by passing command data.

Bulk: This Endpoint is utilized for transfer of large amount of data.

Transfer of large amount of data without loss of any data is important. Extra time time is allowed for this endpoint, if required.

This is used for printer, network card like devices.

isochronous: This endpoint is useful for transferring large amount of audio and video data. Here important thing is continuous flow of data; data lost is accepted during this process.

Interrupt and isochronous endpoints get set to transfer data periodically after specified duration.

USB endpoint gets stored in struct usb_host_endpoint structure and information about this endpoint gets stored in struct usb_endpoint_descriptor.

Some IMP features:

bEndpointAddress: This tells us that data is input or output data.

This gives information that data will go to system or to device.

bmAttributes: This is identified to identify type of endpoint. For example: Bulk, Interrupt, control, isochronous.

wMaxPacketSize: This gives amount of maximum package size handled by the endpoint.

bInterval: Using this we interrupt interval gets identified. (NOT CLEAR, PLEASE LOOK INTO IT.)

Facts:

Endpoints are binde altogether in interface.

Devices can use multiple interfaces at a time. USB interface can have many other settings along with its normal settings.

First of all interface uses typical settings and to perform control using other method they use alternative settings.

This information is stored in usb_interface structure. This interface are binde in form of configuration.

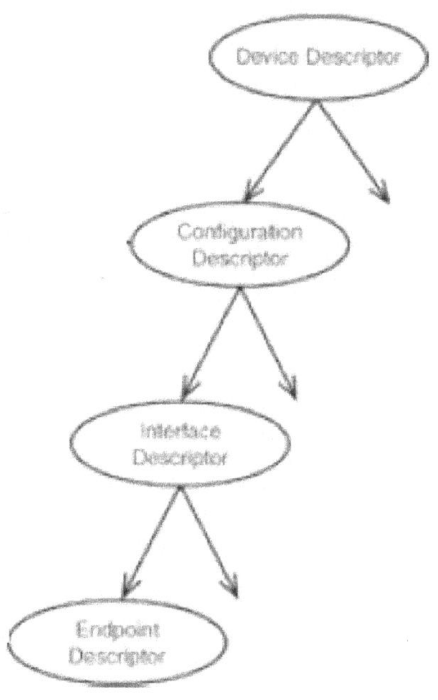

In short configuration means Device Profile.

Interface is a data transfer pipe to transfer device functions and endpoints.

✓ Device has one or more configuration.

✓ Configuration has one or more interface.

✓ Interface has one or more settings.

✓ Interface has one or more endpoints.

First USB device is always root hub. USB core assign one number to root hub. Then port number on which the device is connected. Then configuration number and then interface number.

Example: It will look like: 2-1:1.0

USB Urbs :

Kernel talks with USB devices using USB request block.

USB urbs are useful for data exchange with the endpoint.

URB works as follows:

- USB device driver creates URB.
- Endpoint gets assigned to USB device.
- URB uses device driver to register it in USB core.
- Then USB core register this in USB host controller driver.
- USB host controller processes and transfers USB data.
- Once URB gets completed; USB host controller acknowledges to USB device driver.

USB information Driver:

```c
#include <linux/module.h>
#include <linux/kernel.h>
#include <linux/usb.h>

static struct usb_device *device;

static int pen_probe(struct usb_interface
*interface, const struct usb_device_id
*id)
{
    struct usb_host_interface
*iface_desc;
    struct usb_endpoint_descriptor
*endpoint;
    int i;

    iface_desc = interface-
>cur_altsetting;

    printk (KERN_INFO "Pen i/f %d now
probed:(%04X:%04X)\n",iface_desc-
>desc.bInterfaceNumber, id->idVendor, id-
>idProduct);
    printk(KERN_INFO "ID->bNumEndpoints:
%02X\n",iface_desc->desc.bNumEndpoints);
    printk(KERN_INFO "ID-
>bInterfaceclass: %02X\n", iface_desc-
>desc.bInterfaceClass);
```

```c
        for(i=0; i < iface_desc-
>desc.bNumEndpoints; i++)
        {
                endpoint = &iface_desc-
>endpoint[i].desc;
                printk(KERN_INFO "ED[%d]-
>bEndpointAddress: 0x%02X\n",i, endpoint-
>bEndpointAddress);
                printk(KERN_INFO "ED[%d]-
>bmAttributes: 0x%02X\n", i, endpoint-
>bmAttributes);
                printk(KERN_INFO "ED[%d]-
>wMaxPacketSize: 0x%04X (%d)\n",i,
endpoint->wMaxPacketSize, endpoint->
wMaxPacketSize);
        }
        device =
interface_to_usbdev(interface);
        return 0;
}


static void pen_disconnect(struct
usb_interface *interface)
{
        printk(KERN_INFO "Pen i/f %d now
disconnected \n",interface-
>cur_altsetting->desc.bInterfaceNumber);

}
```

```c
static struct usb_device_id pen_table[]=
{
        { USB_DEVICE(0x0781,0x5567)},
        {}
};
MODULE_DEVICE_TABLE (usb, pen_table);

static struct usb_driver pen_driver =
{
        .name = "pen_driver",
        .id_table = pen_table,
        .probe = pen_probe,
        .disconnect = pen_disconnect,
};

static int __init pen_init(void)
{
        return usb_register(&pen_driver);
}

static void __exit pen_exit(void)
{
        usb_deregister(&pen_driver);
}

module_init(pen_init);
module_exit(pen_exit);

MODULE_LICENSE("GPL");
MODULE_AUTHOR ("MJ");
MODULE_DESCRIPTION("USB PEN Info
DRIVER");
```

In above program we can collect all information which we needed using struct usb_interface handle.

Probe and disconnect runs for interface only and these are the first parameters.

interface_to_usbdev function works as Container device handle.

After running this program we will get all information regarding our device.

Chapter 14

USB device driver File Operation

USB device driver is quite similar to PCI device driver.

As probe function returns `0` means our driver gets registered correctly; if it returns error code that means device does not get registered correctly. Module Device table is useful to automatically detect device and load the driver of that device. Here module.usbmap, madule.pcimap are the map files for USB and PCI.

Data Transfer:

To perform data transfer from pen drive, let's modify the device driver.

In pen drive pen_read and pen_write are two functions used to perform read and write operations in pen drive. We will use usb_bulk_msg() method for data transfer which transfers bulk amount of data. This method use bulk endpoint to transfer data.

Following code will show you to prepare custom device driver having basic read and write features.

USB have two data transfer methods: one method use USB and another method does not need URB because URB gets set automatically inside the function.

Let's learn how to use URB:

> **Using URB:**

Create URB and allocate:

- Here URB gets created first and then it will be allocated.
- struct urb *usb_alloc_urb(int iso_packets, int mem_flags);

- In this function iso_packets parameter will give a count of isochronous packets to transfer.

- If we are not using isochronous method to transfer data then it returns value as '0'.

- mem_flags is a flag similar as we sent flag to kmalloc function.

Submit URB:

- int usb_submit_urb(struct urb *urb, int mem_flags);

- Here pointer and flag of URB will be sent and that URB will be transfer to device.

- One out of three flags will be passed:

- GFP_ATOMIC= this flag will be sent when Caller handles this URB lock and current->state is not TASK_RUNNING state.

- GFP_NOIO = this flag will be sent in case of block IO in patch and storage device error handling part.

- GFP_KERNEL =Else by default flag.

Cancel URB:

- int usb_kill_urb(struct urb *urb);
- int usb_unlink_urb(struct urb *urb);
- usb_kill_urb: Here URB will be closed and device will be disconnected.
- usb_unlink_urb: Here message will be sent to USB core to close URB.

To Free URB:

- Once work is finished; URB tells USB core to free URB.
- void usb_free_urb(struct urb *urb);
- Here we need to pass pointer of URB which needs to free.

To create buffer:

- usb_buffer_alloc(dev->udev, count, GFP_KERNEL, &urb->transfer_dma);
- Using this function we can create buffer for DMA (Direct Memory Access). By this way data will be transfered in fast speed.

void usb_fill_int_urb(struct urb *urb, struct usb_device *dev, unsigned int pipe, void *transfer_buffer, int buffer_length, usb_complete_t complete, void *context, int interval);	Use to include URB in USB core with the help of URB structure. Select function from type of data transfer like Interrupt, bulk, Control
void usb_fill_bulk_urb(struct urb *urb, struct usb_device *dev, unsigned int pipe, void *transfer_buffer, int buffer_length, usb_complete_t complete, void *context);	
void usb_fill_control_urb(struct urb *urb, struct usb_device *dev, unsigned int pipe, unsigned char *setup_packet, void *transfer_buffer, int	

| buffer_ length, usb_complete_t complete, void *context); | |

Simple data transfer without using URB.

int usb_bulk_msg(struct usb_device *usb_dev, unsigned int pipe, void *data, int len, int *actual_length, int timeout);	Bulk message function
int usb_control_msg(struct usb_device *dev, unsigned int pipe, __u8 request, __u8 requesttype, __u16 value, __u16 index, void *data, __u16 size, int timeout);	Control message function

Above functions perform operations related to URB. The functions are easy to use by users to perform data transfer which internally takes care of rest of this. It will make users task easy.

- struct usb_device *usb_dev : Device to which data will be sent.
- unsigned int pipe : Sends or receives end pointer.
  Example: usb_sndbulkpipe, usb_rcvbulkpipe.
- void *data: Pointer of data which receives or sends.
- int len: Length of data buffer
- int *actual_length: Count of actual data count to be sent.
- int timeout : Timeout timer settings.
- __u8 request, __u8 requesttype,__u16 value, __u16 index,void *data, __u16 size : These are control message values for USB message.

Let's see Read function in our program:

```c
static ssize_t pen_read(struct file
*f,char __user *buf , size_t cnt, loff_t
*ppos)
{
    int retval;
    int read_cnt;
    retval =
usb_bulk_msg(device,usb_rcvbulkpipe(devi
ce,BULK_EP_IN),bulk_buf, MAX_PKT_SIZE,
&read_cnt,5000);
    if(retval)
    {
        printk(KERN_ERR "Bulk message
returned %d \n", retval);
        return retval;
    }
    if (copy_to_user(buf, bulk_buf,
MIN(cnt, read_cnt)))
    {
        return -EFAULT;
    }
    return MIN(cnt, read_cnt);
}
```

Here to receive USB data in bulk method parameter has sent to usb_bulk_msg function.

If return value is positive then number of message read is equal to return count.

Data will be written in User buffer using copy_to_user function and is available to user.

In write function first of all data from user buffer will be taken in to bulk buffer with help of copy_from_user function.

Then use sndbulkpipe in usb_bulk_msg function to write data in device.

```c
#include <linux/module.h>
#include <linux/kernel.h>
#include <linux/usb.h>

#define MIN(a,b) (((a) <= (b)) ? (a) :
(b))
#define BULK_EP_OUT 0x01
#define BULK_EP_IN 0x82
#define MAX_PKT_SIZE 512

static struct usb_device *device;
static struct usb_class_driver class;
static unsigned char
bulk_buf[MAX_PKT_SIZE];

static int pen_open(struct inode *i,
struct file *f)
{
    return 0;
}

static int pen_close(struct inode
*i,struct file *f)
{
    return 0;
}

static ssize_t pen_read(struct file
*f,char __user *buf , size_t cnt, loff_t
*ppos)
{
    int retval;
    int read_cnt;
    retval =
usb_bulk_msg(device,usb_rcvbulkpipe(device
,BULK_EP_IN),bulk_buf, MAX_PKT_SIZE,
&read_cnt,5000);
```

```c
if(retval)
    {
          printk(KERN_ERR "Bulk message
returned %d \n", retval);
          return retval;
    }

    if (copy_to_user(buf, bulk_buf,
MIN(cnt, read_cnt)))
    {
          return -EFAULT;
    }
    return MIN(cnt, read_cnt);
}

static ssize_t pen_write(struct file
*f, const char __user *buf, size_t
cnt,loff_t *ppos)
{
    int retval;
    int wrote_cnt
=MIN(cnt,MAX_PKT_SIZE);

    if(copy_from_user(bulk_buf, buf,
MIN(cnt,MAX_PKT_SIZE)))
    {
          return -EFAULT;
    }
    /*write data in to bulk endpoint
*/
    retval
=usb_bulk_msg(device,usb_sndbulkpipe(de
vice,
BULK_EP_OUT),bulk_buf,MIN(cnt,MAX_PKT_S
IZE), &wrote_cnt ,5000);;
```

```c
        if(retval)
        {
                printk(KERN_ERR "Bulk message
returned %d\n", retval);
                return retval;
        }
        return wrote_cnt;
}

static struct file_operations fops =
{
        .open = pen_open,
        .release =pen_close,
        .read =pen_read,
        .write =pen_write,
};
static int pen_probe(struct
usb_interface *interface, const struct
usb_device_id *id)
{
        int retval;

        device = interface_to_usbdev
(interface);

        class.name = "usb/pen%d";
        class.fops = &fops;
        if ((retval
=usb_register_dev(interface, &class )) <
0)
        {
                err("Not abe to get a minor
for this device");
        }
```

```c
        else
        {
            printk(KERN_INFO "Minor
obtained : %d \n", interface->minor);
        }
        return retval;
}

static void pen_disconnect(struct
usb_interface *interface)
{
        usb_deregister_dev(interface,
&class);
}

static struct usb_device_id pen_table[]=
{

        { USB_DEVICE(0x0781,0x5567)},
        {}
};
MODULE_DEVICE_TABLE (usb, pen_table);

static struct usb_driver pen_driver =
{
        .name = "pen_driver",
        .id_table = pen_table,
        .probe = pen_probe,
        .disconnect = pen_disconnect,
};
```

```c
static int __init pen_init(void)
{
     int result;
     if(( result = usb_register
(&pen_driver)))
        {
            err("usb_register failed .err
no %d", result);
        }
     return result;
}

static void __exit pen_exit(void)
{
     usb_deregister(&pen_driver);
}

module_init(pen_init);
module_exit(pen_exit);
MODULE_LICENSE("GPL");
MODULE_AUTHOR ("MJ");
MODULE_DESCRIPTION("USB PEN Device
DRIVER");
```

After running this program and plugging USB pen drive we can observe /dev/pen0 device gets generated.

We can perform some simple read write operations on /dev/pen0. Once we unplug pen drive then /dev/pen0 will get removed.

```
root@ubuntu: /home/shri/mjproj/mjlearn
root@ubuntu:/home/shri/mjproj/mjlearn# sudo insmod pen_driv
er.ko
root@ubuntu:/home/shri/mjproj/mjlearn# dmesg |tail -5
[14123.090750] xhci_hcd 0000:04:00.0: WARN: short transfer
on control ep
[14123.091123] xhci_hcd 0000:04:00.0: WARN: short transfer
on control ep
[14123.091496] xhci_hcd 0000:04:00.0: WARN: short transfer
on control ep
[14123.091832] xhci_hcd 0000:04:00.0: WARN: short transfer
on control ep
[14123.092978] Minor obtained : 0
root@ubuntu:/home/shri/mjproj/mjlearn# ls /dev/pen0
/dev/pen0
root@ubuntu:/home/shri/mjproj/mjlearn# dmesg |tail -5
[14123.091123] xhci_hcd 0000:04:00.0: WARN: short transfer
on control ep
[14123.091496] xhci_hcd 0000:04:00.0: WARN: short transfer
on control ep
[14123.091832] xhci_hcd 0000:04:00.0: WARN: short transfer
on control ep
[14123.092978] Minor obtained : 0
[14177.486166] usb 3-1: USB disconnect, device number 4
root@ubuntu:/home/shri/mjproj/mjlearn# ls /dev/pen0
ls: cannot access /dev/pen0: No such file or directory
root@ubuntu:/home/shri/mjproj/mjlearn#
```

[Note: Before running this program we need to remove usb-storage device driver.]

Important code snippets of USB device driver:

`#include <linux/pci.h>`	This header supports for all USB related information and functions.
`struct usb_driver;`	This structure indicates USB devices.
`struct pci_driver;`	This structure indicates PCI device driver.
`struct usb_device_id;`	Gives Information

	of USB devices supported by driver.
int usb_register(struct usb_driver *d);	Register USB device to USB core.
struct usb_class_driver;	For usb devices which perform communication using major number.
struct urb;	Structure used to send USB data.
struct urb *usb_alloc_urb(int iso_packets, int mem_flags);	To create or remove USB or URB structure.
void usb_free_urb(struct urb *urb);	
int usb_submit_urb(struct	To start or stop USB data

urb *urb, int mem_flags);	transmission.
int usb_kill_urb(struct urb *urb);	
int usb_unlink_urb(struct urb *urb);	
usb_[rcv|snd][ctrl|int|bulk|isoc]pipe()	To create pipe.
usb_buffer_alloc()	Create buffer to perform direct memory transfer.
usb_buffer_free()	Free the buffer once wok will be done.
usb_gadget_register_driver()	Register gadget device.

Gadget Driver:

When embedded system gets connected to computer at that time Linux runs on both computer and on device.

In such cases Computer works as Host and Embedded Device works on Gadget Driver.

It has following types:

Gadget Devices: [Storage, Network] gives answer to request sent by Host.

For example pen drive gives information about its identity as storage class to Host computer.

drivers/usb/gadget/zero.c at this location we can find basic code for gadget driver.

For more information:

- USB skeleton code in Linux system:
    - drivers/usb/usb-skeleton.c
- USB code related document:
    - Documentation/usb/

- Internet source links for USB driver:

    o www.usb.org/developers/docs.

    o www.linux-usb.org.

Chapter 15
Complete USB device driver program.

In Linux some device driver code are structured in standard format so that user can use these codes as a baseline and start programming with help of this baseline.

It is recommend that when programmer start writing new device driver he rather than starting from scratch he should use reference device driver and modify the functions in driver as per need. It makes writing of device driver easy.

Such standard device driver are called as Skeleton Driver. We can find different skeleton drivers like USB skeleton, Framebuffer skeleton in driver folder of Linux.

In this chapter we will be learning about USB skeleton Driver. Here we will go line by line and understand meaning of each functional block.

This will help you to understand complete USB device driver skeleton code.

[Note: Before going further you should read all ious chapters related to USB device driver.]

We can find this driver in the computer at the location: drivers/usb/usb-skeleton.c

We will see 2.2 version of this driver.
Here all program codes are taken as it is intended to explain all code parts. Once you know the entire program then you can change in respective code block to modify the program as per requirement.

```c
#include <linux/kernel.h> // kernel
header to run printk like functions
#include <linux/errno.h>  // contains
error code
#include <linux/init.h>  // process
initialization
#include <linux/slab.h> //to run kmalloc
function.
#include <linux/module.h>  // Help to
write device driver To perform module
related operations.
#include <linux/kref.h> //To track
reference of URB.
#include <linux/uaccess.h> //To use user
to/from functions.
#include <linux/usb.h>  //Contains USB
related functions.
#include <linux/mutex.h> // To set
Mutual semaphore lock.

// We will give Product number and
vender number of a device for which we
will be writing device driver.
// This will be defined in below code
part.

/* Define these values to match your
devices */
#define USB_SKEL_VENDOR_ID     0xfff0
#define USB_SKEL_PRODUCT_ID     0xfff0




// In device table our device gets
registered.
```

```c
// When device with that specific vender
id and product id gets connected to the
system then our driver will
automatically get detected and loaded in
system.

/* table of devices that work with this
driver */
static const struct usb_device_id
skel_table[] = {
    { USB_DEVICE(USB_SKEL_VENDOR_ID,
USB_SKEL_PRODUCT_ID) },
    { }                              /*
Terminating entry */
};
MODULE_DEVICE_TABLE(usb, skel_table);
// Here give Table name and USB as a
parameter.

/* Get a minor range for your devices
from the usb maintainer */
#define USB_SKEL_MINOR_BASE   192  //
Minor number for reference of user.

/* our private defines. if this grows
any larger, use your own .h file */
#define MAX_TRANSFER            (PAGE_SIZE
- 512) // Given Maximum data transfer
limit.
/* MAX_TRANSFER is chosen so that the VM
is not stressed by
   allocations > PAGE_SIZE and the
number of packets in a page
   is an integer 512 is the largest
possible packet on EHCI */
#define WRITES_IN_FLIGHT 8
```

```c
/* arbitrarily chosen */


// This is a Device driver structure in
which all properties of driver will get
defines.
/* Structure to hold all of our device
specific stuff */
struct usb_skel {
    struct usb_device    *udev;
    /* the usb device for this device
*/

    struct usb_interface
    *interface;              /* the
interface for this device */
    struct semaphore    limit_sem;
    /* limiting the number of writes in
progress */
    struct usb_anchor    submitted;
    /* in case we need to retract our
submissions */
    struct urb           *bulk_in_urb;
    /* the urb to read data with */
    unsigned char
*bulk_in_buffer;      /* the buffer to
receive data */
    size_t               bulk_in_size;
    /* the size of the receive buffer
*/

    size_t               bulk_in_filled;
        /* number of bytes in the
buffer */
    size_t               bulk_in_copied;
        /* already copied to user
space */
```

```c
	__u8
	bulk_in_endpointAddr;     /* the
address of the bulk in endpoint */
	__u8
	bulk_out_endpointAddr;    /* the
address of the bulk out endpoint */
	int              errors;
	/* the last request tanked */
	bool             ongoing_read;
	/* a read is going on */
	bool             processed_urb;
	/* indicates we haven't processed
the urb */
	spinlock_t           err_lock;
	/* lock for errors */
	struct kref          kref;
	struct mutex         io_mutex;
	/* synchronize I/O with disconnect
*/
	struct completion
	bulk_in_completion; /* to wait for
an ongoing read */
};
#define to_skel_dev(d) container_of(d,
struct usb_skel, kref)

static struct usb_driver skel_driver;
static void skel_draw_down(struct
usb_skel *dev);


// Below function used to clean all the
things after removing driver.


static void skel_delete(struct kref
*kref)
{
```

```c
    struct usb_skel *dev =
to_skel_dev(kref);

    usb_free_urb(dev->bulk_in_urb);   //
Used to Free URB.
    usb_put_dev(dev->udev); //Device
counter gets reduced by one.
    kfree(dev->bulk_in_buffer);
//Buffer gets free.
    kfree(dev); // Free the device.
}


// Below function runs when device gets
open for function.
static int skel_open(struct inode
*inode, struct file *file)
{
    struct usb_skel *dev; // Device
pointer.
    struct usb_interface *interface; //
Interface pointer.
    int subminor;
    int retval = 0;

    subminor = iminor(inode);

    interface =
usb_find_interface(&skel_driver,
subminor); //To search interfaces in
USB.
    if (!interface) {
        pr_err("%s - error, can't find
device for minor %d\n",
            __func__, subminor);
        retval = -ENODEV;
```

```c
            goto exit;
        }


    dev = usb_get_intfdata(interface);
//Store data of interface.
        if (!dev) {
            retval = -ENODEV;
            goto exit;
        }


    /* increment our usage count for
the device */
        kref_get(&dev->kref);    //Record
that how many times device gets
utilized.
        /* lock the device to allow
correctly handling errors
        * in resumption */
        mutex_lock(&dev->io_mutex);   // Set
mutex lock.


    retval =
usb_autopm_get_interface(interface); //
Device set to Auto suspended mode.


    if (retval)
            goto out_err;


    /* save our object in the file's
private structure */
        file->private_data = dev;     //Fill
interface information in private data of
file.    mutex_unlock(&dev->io_mutex);
//Release themutex lock.


exit:
```

```c
        return retval;
}

// Below code is useful to release the
device.
static int skel_release(struct inode
*inode, struct file *file)
{
        struct usb_skel *dev;

        dev = file->private_data; // Save
the private data.
        if (dev == NULL)
                return -ENODEV;

        /* allow the device to be
autosuspended */
        mutex_lock(&dev->io_mutex); //Set
the lock.
        if (dev->interface)
                usb_autopm_put_interface(dev-
>interface); //Set Auto suspended mode
of device.
        mutex_unlock(&dev->io_mutex);   //
Release the lock.

        /* decrement the count on our
device */
        kref_put(&dev->kref, skel_delete);
//Reduce the count of device by one.
        return 0;
}

// This function is used to read all
errors ,reset all error flags, clean the
memory after opening device.
```

```c
static int skel_flush(struct file *file,
fl_owner_t id)
{
    struct usb_skel *dev;
    int res;

    dev = file->private_data;
    if (dev == NULL)
        return -ENODEV;

    /* wait for io to stop */
    mutex_lock(&dev->io_mutex); //Lock
the mutex.
    skel_draw_down(dev);

    /* read out errors, leave
subsequent opens a clean slate */
    spin_lock_irq(&dev->err_lock);
//Set spin lock.
    res = dev->errors ? (dev->errors ==
-EPIPE ? -EPIPE : -EIO) : 0;
    dev->errors = 0; // read all
errors.
    spin_unlock_irq(&dev->err_lock); //
Release spin lock.

    mutex_unlock(&dev->io_mutex); //
release mutx lock.

    return res;
}


//Following function verifies that data
gets read correctly.
```

```c
 static void
skel_read_bulk_callback(struct urb *urb)
{
     struct usb_skel *dev;

     dev = urb->context;

     spin_lock(&dev->err_lock);
     /* sync/async unlink faults aren't
errors */
     if (urb->status) {
          if (!(urb->status == -ENOENT
||
               urb->status == -ECONNRESET
||
               urb->status == -
ESHUTDOWN))
                    dev_err(&dev->interface-
>dev,
                      "%s - nonzero write
bulk status received: %d\n",
                      __func__, urb-
>status);

          dev->errors = urb->status; //
error got found.
     } else {
          dev->bulk_in_filled = urb-
>actual_length; //Data received
correctly.
     }
     dev->ongoing_read = 0;
     spin_unlock(&dev->err_lock);

     complete(&dev->bulk_in_completion);
// process gets finished.
```

```c
}

//Below function is very usefull in
order to make URB settings to read data.

static int skel_do_read_io(struct
usb_skel *dev, size_t count)
{
    int rv;

    /* prepare a read */
// Fill the data in URB.
    usb_fill_bulk_urb(dev->bulk_in_urb,
            dev->udev,
            usb_rcvbulkpipe(dev-
>udev,
                    dev-
>bulk_in_endpointAddr),
            dev->bulk_in_buffer,
            min(dev->bulk_in_size,
count),
            skel_read_bulk_callback,
            dev);
    /* tell everybody to leave the URB
alone */
    spin_lock_irq(&dev->err_lock);
    dev->ongoing_read = 1;
    spin_unlock_irq(&dev->err_lock);

    /* do it */
//Submit the URB and send data to bulk
end point.
    rv = usb_submit_urb(dev-
>bulk_in_urb, GFP_KERNEL);
    if (rv < 0) {
        dev_err(&dev->interface->dev,
```

```c
                "%s - failed submitting
read urb, error %d\n",
                __func__, rv);
            dev->bulk_in_filled = 0;
            rv = (rv == -ENOMEM) ? rv : -
EIO;
            spin_lock_irq(&dev->err_lock);
            dev->ongoing_read = 0;
            spin_unlock_irq(&dev-
>err_lock);
        }

        return rv;
}


// Following function is to read the
data.
static ssize_t skel_read(struct file
*file, char *buffer, size_t count,
                loff_t *ppos)
{
    struct usb_skel *dev;
    int rv;
    bool ongoing_io;

    dev = file->private_data;

    /* if we cannot read at all, return
EOF */
    if (!dev->bulk_in_urb || !count)
        return 0;

    /* no concurrent readers */
    rv = mutex_lock_interruptible(&dev-
>io_mutex);
```

```c
    if (rv < 0)
        return rv;

    if (!dev->interface) {          /* disconnect() was called */
        rv = -ENODEV;
        goto exit;
    }

    /* if IO is under way, we must not touch things */
retry:
    spin_lock_irq(&dev->err_lock);
    ongoing_io = dev->ongoing_read;
//wait for input output process to finish.
    spin_unlock_irq(&dev->err_lock);

    if (ongoing_io) {
        /* nonblocking IO shall not wait */
        if (file->f_flags & O_NONBLOCK) {
            rv = -EAGAIN;
            goto exit;
        }
        /*
         * IO may take forever
         * hence wait in an interruptible state
         */
        rv = wait_for_completion_interruptible(&dev->bulk_in_completion);
        if (rv < 0)
            goto exit;
```

```c
                /*
                 * by waiting we also
semiprocessed the urb
                 * we must finish now
                 */
            dev->bulk_in_copied = 0;
            dev->processed_urb = 1;
        }

        if (!dev->processed_urb) {
            /*
             * the URB hasn't been
processed
             * do it now
             */
            wait_for_completion(&dev-
>bulk_in_completion);
            dev->bulk_in_copied = 0;
            dev->processed_urb = 1;
        }

        /* errors must be reported */
        rv = dev->errors;
        if (rv < 0) {
            /* any error is reported once
*/
            dev->errors = 0;
            /* to preserve notifications
about reset */
            rv = (rv == -EPIPE) ? rv : -
EIO;
            /* no data to deliver */
            dev->bulk_in_filled = 0;
            /* report it */
            goto exit;
        }
```

```c
	/*
	 * if the buffer is filled we may
satisfy the read
	 * else we need to start IO
	 */

	if (dev->bulk_in_filled) {
		/* we had read data */
		size_t available = dev-
>bulk_in_filled - dev->bulk_in_copied;
		size_t chunk = min(available,
count);

		if (!available) {
			/*
			 * all data has been used
			 * actual IO needs to be
done
			 */
			rv = skel_do_read_io(dev,
count); // Read data.
			if (rv < 0)
				goto exit;
			else
				goto retry;
		}
		/*
		 * data is available
		 * chunk tells us how much
shall be copied
		 */

		if (copy_to_user(buffer,
				dev->bulk_in_buffer
+ dev->bulk_in_copied,
```

```c
                        chunk)) // Store
the data in user memory buffer.
                rv = -EFAULT;
            else
                rv = chunk;

            dev->bulk_in_copied += chunk;

            /*
             * if we are asked for more
than we have,
             * we start IO but don't wait
             */
            if (available < count)
                skel_do_read_io(dev,
count - chunk);
        } else {
            /* no data in the buffer */
            rv = skel_do_read_io(dev,
count);
            if (rv < 0)
                goto exit;
            else if (!(file->f_flags &
O_NONBLOCK))
                goto retry;
            rv = -EAGAIN;
        }
exit:
    mutex_unlock(&dev->io_mutex);
    return rv;
}


// verify that out data gets written
properly or not.
```

```c
static void
skel_write_bulk_callback(struct urb
*urb)
{
	struct usb_skel *dev;

	dev = urb->context;
//Check that error has occurred or not.
	/* sync/async unlink faults aren't
errors */
	if (urb->status) {
		if (!(urb->status == -ENOENT
||
			urb->status == -ECONNRESET
||
			urb->status == -
ESHUTDOWN))
				dev_err(&dev->interface-
>dev,
				"%s - nonzero write
bulk status received: %d\n",
				__func__, urb-
>status);

		spin_lock(&dev->err_lock);
		dev->errors = urb->status;
		spin_unlock(&dev->err_lock);
	}

// Free the DMA buffer once work has
been done.
	/* free up our allocated buffer */
	usb_free_coherent(urb->dev, urb-
>transfer_buffer_length,
			urb->transfer_buffer,
urb->transfer_dma);
```

```c
        up(&dev->limit_sem);
}

\\Function to write the data.
static ssize_t skel_write(struct file
*file, const char *user_buffer,
                  size_t count, loff_t
*ppos)
{
      struct usb_skel *dev;
      int retval = 0;
      struct urb *urb = NULL;
      char *buf = NULL;
      size_t writesize = min(count,
(size_t)MAX_TRANSFER);  //Choose the
minimun number between 'Number of data'
and 'maximum transfer capacity'.

      dev = file->private_data;

      /* verify that we actually have
some data to write */
      if (count == 0) //Check that data
is there or not.
            goto exit;

      /*
       * limit the number of URBs in
flight to stop a user from using up all
       * RAM
       */
      if (!(file->f_flags & O_NONBLOCK))
{
            if (down_interruptible(&dev-
>limit_sem)) {
                  retval = -ERESTARTSYS;
```

```c
                goto exit;
            }
        } else {
            if (down_trylock(&dev-
>limit_sem)) {
                retval = -EAGAIN;
                goto exit;
            }
        }

    spin_lock_irq(&dev->err_lock);
    retval = dev->errors;
    if (retval < 0) {
        /* any error is reported once
*/
        dev->errors = 0;
        /* to preserve notifications
about reset */
        retval = (retval == -EPIPE) ?
retval : -EIO;
    }
    spin_unlock_irq(&dev->err_lock);
    if (retval < 0)
        goto error;

    /* create a urb, and a buffer for
it, and copy the data to the urb */
    urb = usb_alloc_urb(0, GFP_KERNEL);
//Create a URB and allocate the memory
to URB.
    if (!urb) {
        retval = -ENOMEM;
        goto error;
    }
```

```c
    buf = usb_alloc_coherent(dev->udev,
writesize, GFP_KERNEL,
                         &urb-
>transfer_dma); // Perform data transfer
using DMA.
    if (!buf) {
        retval = -ENOMEM;
        goto error;
    }
// Write data from User buffer to device
driver buffer.
    if (copy_from_user(buf,
user_buffer, writesize)) {
        retval = -EFAULT;
        goto error;
    }


    /* this lock makes sure we don't
submit URBs to gone devices */
    mutex_lock(&dev->io_mutex);
    if (!dev->interface) {          /*
disconnect() was called */
        mutex_unlock(&dev->io_mutex);
        retval = -ENODEV;
        goto error;
    }
// To set URB.
    /* initialize the urb properly */
    usb_fill_bulk_urb(urb, dev->udev,
                usb_sndbulkpipe(dev-
>udev, dev->bulk_out_endpointAddr),
                buf, writesize,
skel_write_bulk_callback, dev);
    urb->transfer_flags |=
URB_NO_TRANSFER_DMA_MAP;
```

```c
    usb_anchor_urb(urb, &dev-
>submitted);
//Send data to bulk end point.
    /* send the data out the bulk port
*/
    retval = usb_submit_urb(urb,
GFP_KERNEL);
    mutex_unlock(&dev->io_mutex);
    if (retval) {
        dev_err(&dev->interface->dev,
            "%s - failed submitting
write urb, error %d\n",
            __func__, retval);
        goto error_unanchor;
    }

    /*
     * release our reference to this
urb, the USB core will eventually free
     * it entirely
     */
    usb_free_urb(urb); //Free URB.

    return writesize;

error_unanchor:
    usb_unanchor_urb(urb);
error:
    if (urb) {
        usb_free_coherent(dev->udev,
writesize, buf, urb->transfer_dma);
        usb_free_urb(urb); //Clean
buffer and URB when error occurs.
    }
    up(&dev->limit_sem);
```

```c
exit:
    return retval;
}


// All file-operations of Devices are
defined here .
// All functions mentioned above are
declared below.
.
static const struct file_operations
skel_fops = {
    .owner =   THIS_MODULE,
    .read =          skel_read,
    .write =   skel_write,
    .open =          skel_open,
    .release =       skel_release,
    .flush =   skel_flush,
    .llseek = noop_llseek,
};

/*
 * usb class driver info in order to get
a minor number from the usb core,
 * and to have the device registered
with the driver core
 */
// Name of USB class definition skeleton
and file operation pointer has defined.
static struct usb_class_driver
skel_class = {
    .name =          "skel%d",
    .fops =          &skel_fops,
    .minor_base =  USB_SKEL_MINOR_BASE,
};
```

```c
//Following function is for probe
definition.

static int skel_probe(struct
usb_interface *interface,
                    const struct
usb_device_id *id)
{
    struct usb_skel *dev;
    struct usb_host_interface
*iface_desc;
    struct usb_endpoint_descriptor
*endpoint;
    size_t buffer_size;
    int i;
    int retval = -ENOMEM;

    /* allocate memory for our device
state and initialize it */
    dev = kzalloc(sizeof(*dev),
GFP_KERNEL);
    if (!dev) {
        dev_err(&interface->dev, "Out
of memory\n");
        goto error;
    }
    kref_init(&dev->kref);
    sema_init(&dev->limit_sem,
WRITES_IN_FLIGHT);
    mutex_init(&dev->io_mutex);
    spin_lock_init(&dev->err_lock);
    init_usb_anchor(&dev->submitted);
    init_completion(&dev-
>bulk_in_completion);
```

```c
    dev->udev =
usb_get_dev(interface_to_usbdev(interfac
e));
    dev->interface = interface;

    /* set up the endpoint information
*/
    /* use only the first bulk-in and
bulk-out endpoints */
//Function to search in and out
endpointer.
    iface_desc = interface-
>cur_altsetting;
    for (i = 0; i < iface_desc-
>desc.bNumEndpoints; ++i) {
        endpoint = &iface_desc-
>endpoint[i].desc;

        if (!dev->bulk_in_endpointAddr
&&

usb_endpoint_is_bulk_in(endpoint)) {
            /* we found a bulk in
endpoint */
            buffer_size =
usb_endpoint_maxp(endpoint);
            dev->bulk_in_size =
buffer_size;
            dev->bulk_in_endpointAddr
= endpoint->bEndpointAddress;
            dev->bulk_in_buffer =
kmalloc(buffer_size, GFP_KERNEL);
            if (!dev->bulk_in_buffer)
{
                dev_err(&interface-
>dev,
```

```c
                    "Could not
allocate bulk_in_buffer\n");
                    goto error;
            }
            dev->bulk_in_urb =
usb_alloc_urb(0, GFP_KERNEL);
            if (!dev->bulk_in_urb) {
                dev_err(&interface-
>dev,
                    "Could not
allocate bulk_in_urb\n");
                    goto error;
            }
        }

        if (!dev-
>bulk_out_endpointAddr &&

usb_endpoint_is_bulk_out(endpoint)) {
            /* we found a bulk out
endpoint */
            dev-
>bulk_out_endpointAddr = endpoint-
>bEndpointAddress;
        }
    }
    if (!(dev->bulk_in_endpointAddr &&
dev->bulk_out_endpointAddr)) {
        dev_err(&interface->dev,
            "Could not find both
bulk-in and bulk-out endpoints\n");
        goto error;
    }

    /* save our data pointer in this
interface device */
```

```c
        usb_set_intfdata(interface, dev);

        /* we can register the device now,
as it is ready */
        retval =
usb_register_dev(interface,
&skel_class);
        if (retval) {
                /* something prevented us from
registering this driver */
                dev_err(&interface->dev,
                        "Not able to get a minor
for this device.\n");
                usb_set_intfdata(interface,
NULL);
                goto error;
        }

        /* let the user know what node this
device is now attached to */
        dev_info(&interface->dev,
                "USB Skeleton device now
attached to USBSkel-%d",
                interface->minor);
        return 0;

error:
        if (dev)
                /* this frees allocated memory
*/
                kref_put(&dev->kref,
skel_delete);
        return retval;
}
```

```c
// Below function runs when after pen
drive gets removed from system.
// Here device gets de-register and
allocated memory gets free.

static void skel_disconnect(struct
usb_interface *interface)
{
      struct usb_skel *dev;
      int minor = interface->minor;

      dev = usb_get_intfdata(interface);
      usb_set_intfdata(interface, NULL);

      /* give back our minor */
      usb_deregister_dev(interface,
&skel_class);

      /* prevent more I/O from starting
*/
      mutex_lock(&dev->io_mutex);
      dev->interface = NULL;
      mutex_unlock(&dev->io_mutex);

      usb_kill_anchored_urbs(&dev-
>submitted);

      /* decrement our usage count */
      kref_put(&dev->kref, skel_delete);

      dev_info(&interface->dev, "USB
Skeleton #%d now disconnected", minor);
}

// Timer counter function.
```

```c
static void skel_draw_down(struct
usb_skel *dev)
{
    int time;

    time =
usb_wait_anchor_empty_timeout(&dev-
>submitted, 1000);
    if (!time)
        usb_kill_anchored_urbs(&dev-
>submitted);
    usb_kill_urb(dev->bulk_in_urb);
}
```

```c
// Device will be closed after some time
and this feature saves the power when
the device is not utilized.
```

```c
static int skel_suspend(struct
usb_interface *intf, pm_message_t
message)
{
    struct usb_skel *dev =
usb_get_intfdata(intf);

    if (!dev)
        return 0;
    skel_draw_down(dev);
    return 0;
}
```

```c
//Device gets resumed whenever needed.
 static int skel_resume(struct
usb_interface *intf)
{
    return 0;
```

```c
}

//Function to reset device and save
device state.
static int skel_pre_reset(struct
usb_interface *intf)
{
	struct usb_skel *dev =
usb_get_intfdata(intf);

	mutex_lock(&dev->io_mutex);
	skel_draw_down(dev);

	return 0;
}

//After device resumes from reset
provide the previous state information
of device.
static int skel_post_reset(struct
usb_interface *intf)
{
	struct usb_skel *dev =
usb_get_intfdata(intf);

	/* we are sure no URBs are active -
no locking needed */
	dev->errors = -EPIPE;
	mutex_unlock(&dev->io_mutex);

	return 0;
}


// USB device driver definition.
static struct usb_driver skel_driver = {
	.name =		"skeleton",
```

```c
    .probe =   skel_probe,
    .disconnect =   skel_disconnect,
    .suspend =      skel_suspend,
    .resume = skel_resume,
    .pre_reset =    skel_pre_reset,
    .post_reset =   skel_post_reset,
    .id_table =     skel_table,
    .supports_autosuspend = 1,
};

module_usb_driver(skel_driver);

MODULE_LICENSE("GPL");
```

Yeah! We have gone through complete program of USB Device driver. Now correlate our learning with this practical implementation

You can also modify this code to develop USB device driver for your own product.

Chapter 16
USB 3.0 Special

By improving many aspects of USB 2.0 new version of USB has arrived in market called as USB 3.0.

USB3.0 is also called as superfast USB.This is specially designed to transfer bidirectional data. Because of this data transfer rate gets increased by 10 times.

One more speciality of USB 3.0 is that USB 3.0 devices support for USB 2.0 also. This means that they have backward compatibility.

USB 3.0 port looks like USB 2.0 port but it has blue strip inside of USB connection port by using which we can identify USB 3.0 port.

USB 3.0 Port connection:

USB 3.0 has total 9 pins, 4 pins are same as in USB 2.0, two pairs of pins are added for fast data transfer and one extra ground pin is also added in USB 3.0.

Using these pins we can send more information and can connect to multiple devices.

How USB pins goes from cable is shown in the diagram below:

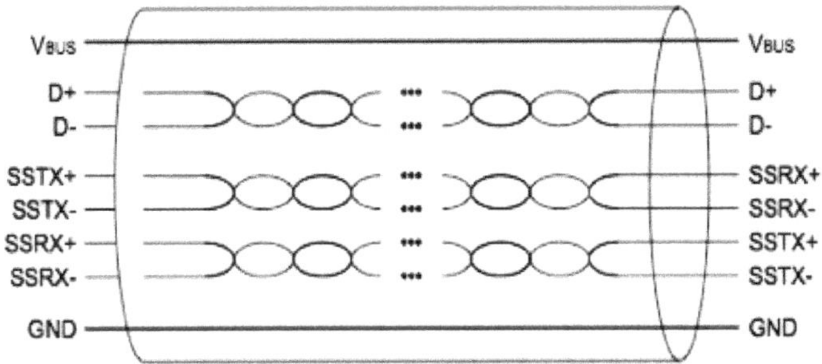

USB 2.0 and USB 3.0 have data +, data -, power and ground pins.

Using pair of SSTX and SSRX transmitter and receiver lines we can perform bidirectional data transfer with dedicated lines.

All upcoming USB devices will have USB 3.0 port . We will also be ready to update our device driver to support USB 3.0.

Let's learn about what changes we need to perform in device driver structure to support USB 3.0 devices.

Bulk endpoint streaming:

Bulk Endpoint streaming is a newly added special feature of USB 3.0 Device Driver to perform data transfer.

Using this device driver we can bind multiple end points into one and perform at a time multiple data transfer serially. In this way multiple data will be sent at the same time.

How to incorporate this feature in driver?

When buffer is in queue of stream ring then the device will know that the data of that stream ID is ready to transfer. Device will provide information to host about which stream to start.

USB 3.0 Special

Following driver code needs to modify:

```
int usb_alloc_streams(struct
usb_interface *interface, struct
usb_host_endpoint **eps, unsigned int
num_eps, unsigned int num_streams,
gfp_t mem_flags);
```

The device driver will call API to request host controller to allocate memory.

So that driver can use num_streams amount of stream ID's.

ID of Similar stream should pass to setup array of usb_host_endpoint. Each endpoint in super speed device gives information about maximum stream ID's it can handle. It is necessary to call usb_free_streams() function every time. Device driver can use above API for only once for one endpoint. After that, endpoint should make free by calling usb_free_streams() function when all task are finished.

How to use new stream ID?

Stream ID '0' is reserved and therefore do not use this ID for data communication. If usb_alloc_streams() function returns N values than we can use stream from number 1 to number N.

Clean operation:

We can stop using stream. In that case we have to use following function to stop communication.

```
void usb_free_streams(struct
usb_interface *interface, struct
usb_host_endpoint **eps, unsigned int
num_eps, gfp_t mem_flags);
```

When driver releases interface, all the stream IDs will get de-allocated. By doing this, endpoint will open to use other drivers which are not able to use stream.

In this way we can use bulk end point feature of device driver to perform fast data transfer using USB 3.0.

...Be ready for NextGen Devices...

Chapter 17
Device Driver Lock

In our computer many process are running at a time; many times multiple thread works on same memory area.

In such cases if memory management is not proper then there may be deadlock or conflict, which may result in to system hang or system crash.

Mutual Exclusion:

- Before using particular piece of memory, check that no one else is using that memory.
- When our program is using a particular piece of memory, lock the memory in order to prevent others to use it.
- This is known as Locking or Mutual Exclusion.

Locking has two major types: Semaphore Lock and Spin Lock.

Semaphore Lock:

This lock allows using only one resource at a time and is called as Sleeping Lock.

When we want to lock we need to give down() command and then perform our task on data. Once our task iscompleted then give up() command to release the lock. After this the resource will be open for other processes to use it further.

If our process needs one resource which gets locked by other process then our process goes in to sleep mode.

When the required resource gets free then our process wake up from sleep and use semaphore to take control of required resource.

Special type of semaphore is known as **Mutex.** It works in binary (1/0) mode. It has only two operational states (lock /unlock).

This means that only one task can be locked at a time. But semaphore can handle multiple tasks at the same time.

- First of all Mutex needs to be initialized.

- static DECLARE_MUTEX(my_lock);

- Then use **down** command to lock resource.

- Down function reduce semaphore value by one.

- down(&my_lock);

- Then perform the work on that resource.

- Then use 'up' command to release lock.

- up(&my_lock);

Spin Lock:

Semaphore saves the resource from process which works at a time on single resource.

Spin lock is not a sleeping Lock. It saves critical section memory from interference by other programs.

If some function does not get locked then it waits there only. In this case NOP (no operation) command starts running. During this time processor does not perform any other task. It is recommended to keep spin lock duration at low. It will reduce many problems which may occur while performing spin lock.

In kernel, many times, Spin lock is used. It performs very well in programs like interrupt handler.

If another functions acquired a lock then code goes in a loop during this and checks if the lock is released. The process is known as spin.

Spin lock is very useful in Multiprocessor systems.

Spin lock function is defined in <linux/spinlock.h> header file.

Spin lock gets declared as given below:

- struct spinlock my_lock;

- spin_lock_init(&my_spin_lock);

- Spin lock is acquired by using following function:

    - spin_lock(&my_lock);

- Spin lock gets released by using following function:

    - spin_unlock(&my_lock);

- We can use spin lock to save our data from interrupt running in another process.

We have learnt about use of locks while writing device driver. We have already seen how to use these locks in USB Program chapter under USB skeleton section.

Go back once again and look in to USB skeleton driver and observe how these locks come into practices.

Chapter 18
Display Device Driver

Video device creates visual output data to display content on screen.

Linux video system is based on Frame buffer layers. Using this hardware, independent driver system is created.

Video graphics card can be of different hardware type. Hence we might need to perform different coding for different hardwares. To avoid this problem, frame buffer layer is created in Linux. Application can be run on different hardware platforms by using this feature without doing any changes in the application.

Many web browsesr, video players like applications use direct frame buffer to perform graphics hardware related data transfer operations.

Frame buffer concept:

As shown in the image below, Movie player uses common frame buffer API to perform data transfer on different video cards. From this example you will understand the importance and usefulness of the Frame buffer.

Some applications like x-windows can directly communicate with hardware without using API.

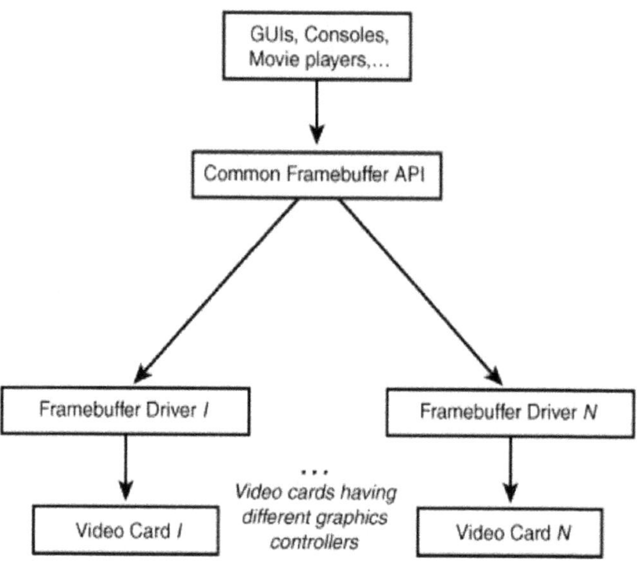

When we enter fbset command in terminal window we can see display settings applied by frame buffer driver. It contains details information regarding display Resolution, Frequency, Timing, Vertical Sync, and Horizontal Sync.

- Command to install fbset utility package:
  apt-get install fbset

Frame buffer API:

We need to know about some important data structure when using frame buffer API.

1) struct fb_var_screeninfo: This structure contains some setting which can be changed.
Example: Resolution and Margins settings can be changed by programmer.

2) struct fb_fix_screeninfo:This data structure contains fix information about video hardware.
Example: Frame buffer memory size and starting address.

3) fb_cmap: This defines color map of frame buffer. User can define number of red, blue, green [RGB] colors.

This also contains feature to set transparency.

Framebufer Driver:

Here we will communicate with our display using frame buffer driver. We will interact with frame buffer memory location so that display will show changed content on screen.

In this way, data in frame buffer memory will be seen on screen.

Data Structure:

struct fb_info: This is main data structure in frame buffer device driver. This structure is defined in include/linux/fb.h.

```c
struct fb_info
{
/* ... */
struct fb_var_screeninfo var; /*
Variable screen information.

struct fb_fix_screeninfo fix; /* Fixed
screen information.

/* ... */
struct fb_cmap cmap; /* Color map.

/* ... */
struct fb_ops *fbops; /* Driver
operations.

/* ... */
char __iomem *screen_base; /* Frame
buffer's virtual address */
unsigned long screen_size; /* Frame
buffer's size */
/* ... */
/* From here on everything is device
dependent */
void *par; /* Private area */
};
```

In the above structure we can see screen fix info, variable info, and color map like data structures. We can also see fb_ops structure which is used in file operation.

Screen buffer size and base address is defined in the above structure.

Data related to driver is stored here in par pointer.

We can allocate memory for fb_info using framebuffer_alloc() method .

fb_ops structure:

fb_ops structure gives entry point for framebufer driver. Some of the functions are necessary to run and some are optional.

Optional functions are related to graphics.

We can see fb_ops structure as shown below:

```c
struct fb_ops
{
    struct module *owner;
    /* Open Driver */
    int (*fb_open)(struct fb_info *info,
    int user);
    /* Close the driver */
    int (*fb_release)(struct fb_info
    *info, int user);
    /* using variable screeninfo check
    that device parameter are correct or
    not.*/
    int (*fb_check_var)(struct
    fb_var_screeninfo *var,
    struct fb_info *info);
    /* Set register of video
    controller*/
    int (*fb_set_par)(struct fb_info
    *info);
    /* Set color register parameter. */
    int (*fb_setcolreg)(unsigned regno,
    unsigned red,
    unsigned green, unsigned blue,
    unsigned transp, struct fb_info
    *info);
    /* Make display blank */
    int (*fb_blank)(int blank, struct
    fb_info *info);
```

```c
    /* Following method uses Graphics
    card for operation. */

    /* Fill up rectangle area by
    pixels*/
    void (*fb_fillrect)(struct fb_info
    *info,const struct fb_fillrect
    *rect);
    /* Copy some part of reactangle from
    one location to another location.*/
    void (*fb_copyarea)(struct fb_info
    *info,const struct fb_copyarea
    *region);
    /* Draw image on screen */
    void (*fb_imageblit)(struct fb_info
    *info,const struct fb_image *image);
    /* To rotate display */
    void (*fb_rotate)(struct fb_info
    *info, int angle);
    /* IO select interface command
    related to device. */
    int (*fb_ioctl)(struct fb_info
    *info, unsigned int cmd,
    unsigned long arg);
/* ... */
};
```

To check and set Parameter:

fb_check_var(): This method performs basic operation on device. It also checks resolution bit per pixel value and sets RGB format.

fb_set_par(): This method sets register settings in LCD controller. It includes margin settings. Also size_reg contains resolution settings and DMA gets set in DMA_REG, which is further utilized in direct memory access.

Color Mode:

Psudo color and true color are two types of color mode. We can save the frame buffer memory space by making color value as index rather than pixel value. For this our hardware should support color set [palette].

LCD has 16 bit/pixel and RGB565 format.

That means fb_check_var() function takes bit offset value for red, green, bule as 11, 5, 0.

[0-5 (5): Blue, 5-11(6): Green, 11-16[5]: Red]

fb_set_par() function uses Alfa Blending technique to mix pixel value and background. Bit length [5+6+11=16] used by RGB to encode is called as color depth. Using this frame buffer displays boot logo image on our computer screen.

Screen Blanking:

fb_blank() This function supports display blanking and un-blanking. This feature is used for power management.

Use setterm -blank 10 command to make our display blank for 10 minutes.

This command sets value for blanking in CTRL_REG register and call fb_blank() function. After calling this function, display goes blank.

Accelerated Method:

Accelerated methods are used for performing video and graphics intensive operations.

To blend, streat or to move the bitmap, we need graphics hardware in our system.

In fb_ops we have already seen list of accelerated methods.

Here user can take benefit of special features and facility provided by Graphics card to see good quality image on screen.

fb_imageblit() method creates image on display.

If our system does not have any graphics card then frame buffer driver use simple method of cfb_imageblit() to perform this task.

cfb_imageblit() method does not use power of graphics hardware.

This function is used when we form a boot image on screen.

fb_copyarea() function is used to copy some part of screen from one location to other location.

fb_fillrect() function fill some part of screen by pixel lines.

Use of Direct Memory access by Framebuffer:

DMA engine takes frame data from system memory and processes it using processor and shows the graphics content on screen.

Rate of DMA depends on refresh rate of display.

myfb_probe() function is used to reserve coherent frame buffer DMA access.

In that function dma_alloc_coherent() method is used.

myfb_set_par() method writes DMA address in DMA_REG register of controller.

When driver starts DMA using myfb_enable_controller() function then controller uses Direct memory access and takes pixel data directly from framebuffer and displays the pixel content on screen.

Contrast and Brightness:

LCD controller uses CONTRAST_REG register to set contrast.

Processor uses general purpose input output lines to control brightness.

User can control backlight with backlight_device_register() register.

Visit below links to further study Display driver:

- Linux framebuffer project link:

  o www.linux-fbdev.org

- Framebuffer driver location in our Linux system:

  o drivers/video/*fb.c

- Frame buffer skeleton driver:

  o drivers/video/*fb.c

Display Driver summary:

Table below provides important functions of display driver to provide kernel interface.

register_framebuffer()	Register frame buffer device.
unregister_framebuffer()	Free frame buffer device.

framebuffer_alloc()	Allocate memory for fb_info structure.
framebuffer_release()	Free the allocated memory.
fb_alloc_cmap()	Allocate color map.
fb_dealloc_cmap()	Free color map.
dma_alloc_coherent()	Allocate the memory using DMA mapping.
dma_free_coherent()	Free DMA buffer memory.

Chapter 19
Memory Allocation

Device drivers have to be careful when using memory. Most device drivers allocate kernel, non-paged, memory to hold their data.

Linux provides kernel memory allocation and deallocation routines and are used by device drivers.

- ✓ The kernel usually wants physically contiguous memory.
- ✓ Often, the kernel must allocate the memory without sleeping.
- ✓ Mistakes in the kernel have a much higher price than they do elsewhere.
- ✓ Understanding of memory related issues can help us to handle process relatively painless.

Some device drivers have to be aware of the existence of memory zones. In addition, many drivers need the services of memory-allocation functions.

Kmalloc:

The kernel organizes physical memory into pages. The page size depends on the architecture. On x86-based machines, it's 4096 bytes.

kmalloc() is a memory-allocation function that returns contiguous memory from ZONE_NORMAL (16MB-896MB).

Note: ZONE_NORMAL is normally addressable region also called as low memory.

When you have finished accessing the memory allocateed via kmalloc(), you must return it to the kernel. This job is done using kfree().

Prototype:

```
#include <linux/slab.h>

void *kmalloc(size_t size, int
flags);
```

First parameter (size_t size) indicates allocation size in bytes.It indicates size of the block to be allocated.

flags is a mode specifier. All supported flags are listed in include/linux./gfp.h (get free pages), but these are the commonly used ones.

- GFP_KERNEL: Used by process context code to allocate memory. If this flag is specified, kmalloc() is allowed to go to sleep and wait for pages to get freed up.
- GFP_ATOMIC: Used by interrupt context code to get hold of memory. In this mode, kmalloc() is not allowed to sleep-wait for free pages, so the probability of successful allocation with GFP_ATOMIC is lower than with GFP_KERNEL.
- GFP_DMA: Allocate only DMA-capable memory.

Upon successful return, kmalloc() returns a pointer to size bytes of memory.

Because memory returned by kmalloc() retains the contents from its previous allocation settings, there could be a security risk if it's exposed to user space.

To get zeroed kmalloced memory, use kzalloc().

kernel manages the system's physical memory, which is available only in page sized chunks.

Linux handles memory allocation by creating a set of pools of memory objects of fixed sizes.

Remember: kernel can allocate only certain predefined, fixed-size byte arrays.

Smallest allocation that kmalloc can handle is as big as 32 or 64 bytes and Highest allocation is up to 128 KB.

Kernel does implement a facility to create some special pools for same size high-volume objects, which is often called a lookaside cache.

The cache manager in the Linux kernel is sometimes called the "slab allocator." For that reason, its functions and types are declared in <linux/slab.h>.

```kmem_cache_t *kmem_cache_create(char *name, size_t size, size_t offset, unsigned long flags, constructor( ), destructor( ));```	Creates and destroys a slab cache. The cache can be used to allocate several objects of the same size.
```int kmem_cache_destroy(kmem_ca che_t *cache);```	
```void *kmem_cache_alloc(kmem_cac he_t *cache, int flags);```	Allocates and releases a single object from the cache.
```void kmem_cache_free(kmem_cache _t *cache, const void *obj);```	

Note: kernel developers create an abstraction known as a memory pool ("mempool").

A memory pool is really just a form of a lookaside cache that tries to always keep a list of free memory around for use in emergencies.

Get_free_page:

`get_zeroed_page(unsigned int flags);`	Returns a pointer to a new page and fills the page with zeros.
`__get_free_page(unsigned int flags);`	Similar to get_zeroed_pag e but doesn't clear the page.
`__get_free_pages(unsigne d int flags, unsigned int order);`	Allocates and returns a pointer to the first byte of a memory area

	that is physically contiguous pages long but doesn't zero the area.

vmalloc:

If you need to allocate large memory buffers, and you don't require the memory to be physically contiguous, use vmalloc() rather than kmalloc().

vmalloc() enjoys bigger allocation size limits than kmalloc() but is slower and can't be called from interrupt context.

Prototypes of the function:

```
#include <linux/vmalloc.h>

void *vmalloc(unsigned long
size);

void vfree(void * addr);
```

vmalloc() allocates a connecting memory region in the virtual address space.

Although the pages are not serial in physical memory, the kernel sees them as an attached range of addresses.

Memory allocated with vmalloc is released by vfree in the same way as that of kfree.

High-performance network drivers commonly use vmalloc() to allocate large descriptor rings when the device is opened.

Note:

- Memory obtained from vmalloc is slightly less efficient to work with.
- You cannot use the physically discontiguous memory returned by vmalloc() to perform Direct Memory Access (DMA).
- vmalloc is not different in how it uses the hardware, but rather in how the kernel performs the allocation task.

Ioremap:

To remap I/O memory into kernel address space ioremap is used.

Like vmalloc, ioremap builds new page tables and map memory space but it doesn't actually allocate any memory.

ioremap is most useful for mapping the (physical) address of a PCI buffer to (virtual) kernel space.

Regions mapped with ioremap are freed with iounmap.

Iounmap: Unmap I/O memory from kernel address space.

```
#include <asm/io.h>

void * ioremap(unsigned long offset,
unsigned long size);

void iounmap(void *addr);
```

Parameters:

- phys_addr: Begin of physical address range
- size: size of physical address range
- Returns: virtual start address of mapped range

No real mapping is done here. Only the virtual address is returned.

Chapter 20
Interrupt Handling

An interrupt is simply a signal that the hardware can send when it wants the processor's attention.

Because of the indeterminate nature of I/O, and speed mismatches between I/O devices and the processor, devices request the processor's attention by asserting certain hardware signals asynchronously. These hardware signals are called interrupts.

Each interrupting device is assigned an associated identifier called an interrupt request (IRQ) number.

When the processor detects that an interrupt has been generated on an IRQ, it abruptly stops what it is doing and invokes an interrupt service routine (ISR) registered for the corresponding IRQ.

ISRs are critical pieces of code that directly converses with the hardware. They are given the privilege of instant execution in the larger interest of system performance.
Interrupt handlers (ISRs) execute in interrupt context.

The kernel accomplishes useful work using a combination of process contexts and interrupt contexts. Interrupt handlers run asynchronously in interrupt context.

Kernel code running in interrupt context is always runs to completion and is not preemptible. Because of this, there are restrictions on what can be done from interrupt context.

Code executing from interrupt context cannot do the following:

- Go to sleep or relinquish the processor
- Acquire a mutex
- Perform time-consuming tasks
- Access user space virtual memory

Implementation of interrupt registration interface:

Calls that register and unregister an interrupt handler.

```
#include <linux/interrupt.h>

int request_irq(unsigned int irq,
irqreturn_t (*handler)( ), unsigned
long flags, const char *dev_name, void
*dev_id);

void free_irq(unsigned int irq, void
*dev_id);
```

- unsigned int irq : The interrupt number being requested.
- irqreturn_t (*handler)(int, void *, struct pt_regs *) : The pointer to the handling function being installed.
- unsigned long flags : a bit mask of options related to interrupt management.
- const char *dev_name :The string passed to request_irq is used in /proc/interrupts to show the owner of the interrupt.

- void *dev_id :Pointer used for shared interrupt lines. It is a unique identifier that is used when the interrupt line is freed and that may also be used by the driver to point to its own private data area.

- Value returned from request_irq to the requesting function is either 0 to indicate success or a negative error code to indicate failure.

Bits that can be set in flags are as follows:

✓ SA_INTERRUPT: Indicates a "fast" interrupt handler. Fast handlers are executed with interrupts disabled on the current processor.

✓ SA_SHIRQ: Interrupt can be shared between devices.

✓ SA_SAMPLE_RANDOM: These devices return truly random numbers when read and are designed to help application software choose secure keys for encryption.

The correct place to call request_irq is when the device is first opened, before the hardware is instructed to generate interrupts.

The place to call free_irq is the last time the device is closed, after the hardware is told not to interrupt the processor any more.

When your driver unloads, you need to unregister your interrupt handler and potentially disable the interrupt line.

Freeing an IRQ is done as follows:

```
free_irq(int irq, void *dev_id);
```

This method unregister a given interrupt handler; if no handlers now exist on the line, the given interrupt line is disabled.

Proc interface:

Whenever a hardware interrupt reaches the processor, an internal counter is incremented, providing a way to check whether the device is working as expected.

The /proc/interrupts display shows how many interrupts have been delivered to each CPU on the system.

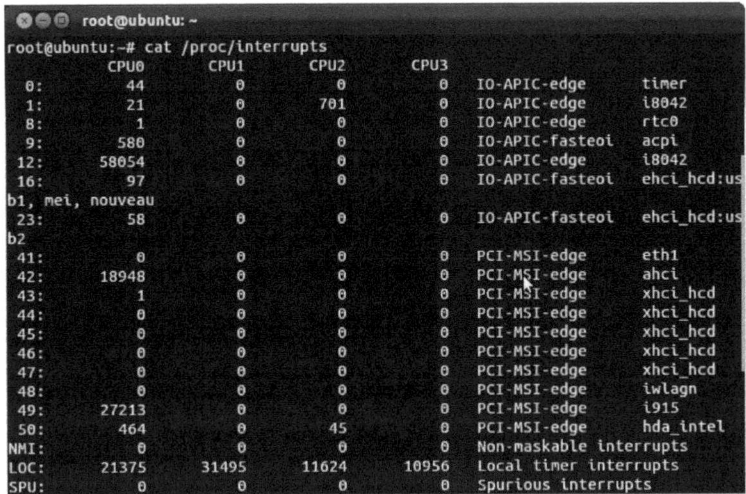

1. First columan is IRQ number, it Indicates the interrupt line. On this system, interrupts numbered 0, 1, 8, 12, and 16 are present.

2. The second column is a counter of the number of interrupts received. A column is

present for each processor on the system (CPU 0 to CPU 3)

3. The third column is the interrupt controller handling this interrupt.

4. Finally, the last column is the device associated with this interrupt. This name is supplied by the devname parameter to request_irq().

Path of interrupt through hardware and kernel:

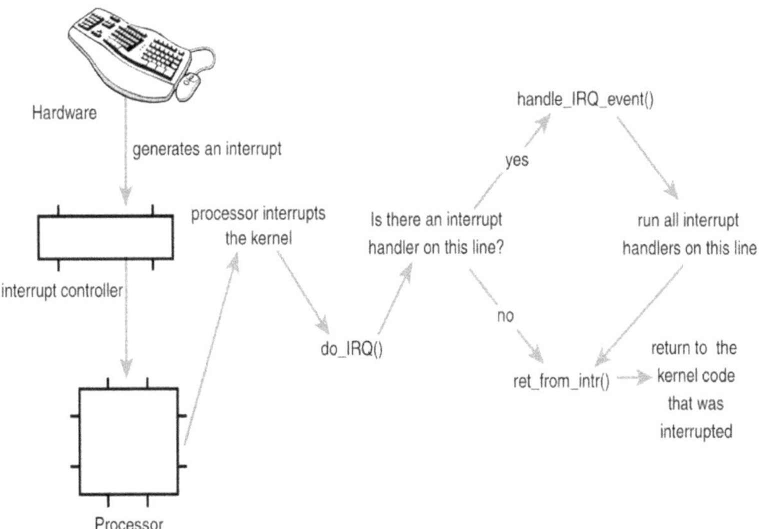

When an interrupt occurs, the processor looks if interrupts are masked. If they are, nothing happens until they are unmasked. When interrupts become unmasked, if there are any pending interrupts, the processor picks one.

Then the processor executes the interrupt by branching to a particular address in memory. The code at that address is called the interrupt handler. When the processor branches there, it masks interrupts and saves the contents of registers in some other registers.

When the handler finishes executing, it executes a special return-from-interrupt instruction that restores the saved registers and unmasks interrupts.

Programming Tips:

- ✓ For protecting critical sections inside interrupt handlers should use spinlocks.
- ✓ Interrupt handlers cannot directly exchange data with user space.
- ✓ Interrupt handlers are supposed to get out of the way quickly once job is done.
- ✓ Interrupt handlers can be interrupted by handlers associated with IRQs that have higher priority.
- ✓ Asynchronous interrupts generated by external hardware.
- ✓ The processor itself generates Synchronous interrupts by executing an instruction.
- ✓ Device drivers have to connect their IRQ number to an interrupt handler.
- ✓ Driver initialization is not a good place for requesting an IRQ.
- ✓ The IRQ is freed when the application closes the device and not while exiting the driver module.

Softirqs, Tasklets, and WorkQueues:

Interrupt handlers are designed in two parts:

The upper half of a driver comprises all the parts that are invoked as a result of user process calls.

Driver entry points that execute in response to open(), close(), ioctl(), mmap(), read() and write().

The lower half of a driver comprises the code that is called to respond to a hardware interrupt. An interrupt can occur at almost any time, including large parts of the time when the kernel is executing other services, including driver upper halves, and even driver lower halves for devices with lower-priority interrupts.

A top half that interacts with the hardware, and a bottom half that does most of the processing with all interrupts enabled.

Bottom halves are synchronous because the kernel decides when to execute them.

The following mechanisms are available in the kernel to defer work to a bottom half: softirqs, tasklets, and work queues.

	Softirqs	Tasklets	Work Queues
Deferred work runs in	Interrupt context.	Interrupt context.	Process context
Can run simultaneously On	Different CPUs.	Different CPUs and Different CPUs can run different Tasklets.	Different CPUs.
Sleep	Cannot sleep.	Cannot sleep	May Sleep
Scheduled	Cannot be scheduled	Cannot be scheduled	May be scheduled
Ease of use	Not easy.	Easy to use.	Easy to use.
Use If deferred work-	Does not go to sleep and have crucial scalability or speed requirements	Does not go to sleep.	May go to sleep.

Chapter 21

I/O Control

Introducing ioctl() :

This routine is used to receive and implement application commands that request device-specific actions.

- ✓ Common char driver method is called I/O Control.
- ✓ Most common hardware-controlling operation is ioctl.
- ✓ Input/Output Control is a common operation, or system call, available in most driver categories.

If there is no other system call that meets a particular requirement, then ioctl() is the one to use.

Example: Volume control for an audio device, display configuration for a video device, reading device registers.

The ioctl() function implementation does a switch case over the commmand to implement the corresponding functionality.

Every device can have its own ioctl commands, which can be read ioctl's (to send information from a process to the kernel), write ioctl's (to return information to a process. The ioctl function is called with three parameters: the file descriptor of the appropriate device file, the ioctl number, and a parameter, which is of type long.

Prototype:

```
int ioctl(int fd, unsigned long
cmd, ...);
```

- Dots in the prototype represent a single optional argument.
- Fd is file descriptor.

#include <linux/ioctl.h>: Declares all the macros used to define ioctl commands.

To choose ioctl numbers for your driver you should first check include/asm/ioctl.h and Documentation/ioctl-number.txt.

The ioctl number encodes the major device number, the type of the ioctl, the command, and the type of the parameter.

This ioctl number is usually created by a macro call (_IO, _IOR, _IOW or _IOWR --- depending on the type) in a header file.

This header file should then be included both by the programs which will use ioctl (so they can generate the appropriate ioctl's) and by the kernel module (so it can understand it).

The implementation of ioctl is usually a switch statement based on the command Number.

If an inappropriate ioctl command has been issued, then -ENOTTY error should be returned. This error code is interpreted by the C library as "inappropriate ioctl for device".

Stepwise execution of ioctl:

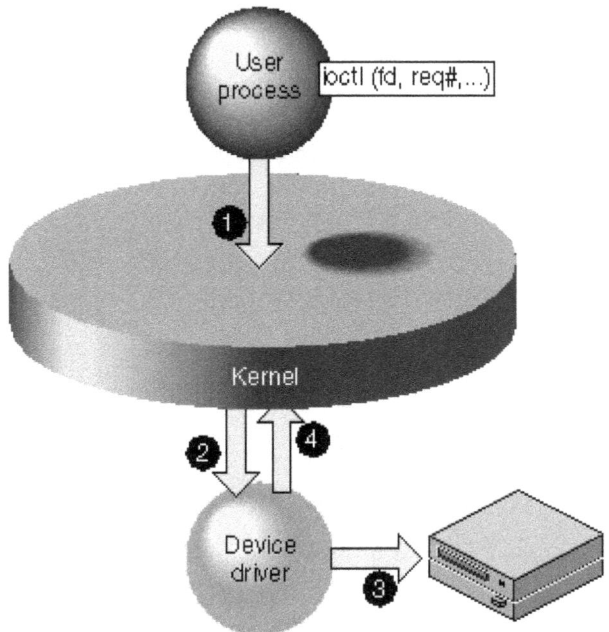

The steps illustrated in Figure are:

1. The user process calls the ioctl() kernel function, passing the file descriptor from open and one or more other parameters.

2. The kernel uses the major device number to select the device driver, and calls the device driver, passing the minor device number, the request number, and an optional third parameter from ioctl().

3. The device driver interprets the request number and other parameter, notes changes in its own data structures, and possibly issues commands to the device.
4. The device driver returns an exit code to the kernel, and the kernel (then or later) redispatches the user process.

Note:

- The user process is not allowed to issue ioctl() for a block device.
- The interpretation of ioctl request codes and parameters is entirely up to the device driver.

Use following commands to get information regarding ioctl:

```
root@ubuntu:~# man -k ioctl
addpart (8)              - simple wrapper around the "add partition" ioctl
blockdev (8)             - call block device ioctls from the command line
console_ioctl (4)        - ioctl's for console terminal and virtual consoles
delpart (8)              - simple wrapper around the "del partition" ioctl
ioctl (2)                - control device
ioctl_list (2)           - list of ioctl calls in Linux/i386 kernel
tty_ioctl (4)            - ioctls for terminals and serial lines
root@ubuntu:~# info ioctl
root@ubuntu:~#
```

man Command: It is used to access the manual pages for thousands of utilities. Default location: is /usr/share/man. man is the traditional form of help for almost every command on your system

Info Command: Another common form of Linux documentation is created using texinfo tool which can be accessed by using info command. Default location:/usr/share/info.

info is an alternative system to provide manual refrence pages for commands.

Chapter 22
Sample Programs

The complete "memory" Driver:

In this topic we will see example of building complete device driver called as memory.c.

This is simple device driver which will allow a character to be read from or written into it.

To develop this driver we need to add some #include statements as below.

<memory initial> =

```
/* Necessary includes for device drivers */
#include <linux/init.h>
#include <linux/config.h>
#include <linux/module.h>
#include <linux/kernel.h> /* printk() */
#include <linux/slab.h> /* kmalloc() */
#include <linux/fs.h> /* everything... */
#include <linux/errno.h> /* error codes */
#include <linux/types.h> /* size_t */
```

After the #include files we will declare functions which will be defined later.

The common file related functions are declared in file_operations structure.

Initialization and exit functions are used for loading and removing the module.

Finally, two global variables of the driver are declared: one is the major number of the driver and other is a memory pointer memory_buffer, which will be used as storage for the driver data.

Connection of device with files:

Devices are accessed from user space in as files. These device files are normally subdirectories of the /dev directory.

To link device files with a kernel module major number and minor number are used. kernel uses major number to link a file with its driver. The minor number is for internal use of the device.

Device file must be created by following command with root login:

✓ # mknod /dev/memory c 60 0

Here, c is char device is to be created, 60 is major number and 0 is minor number.

register_chrdev function is used to link driver with its corresponding /dev file.

It is called with three arguments: major number, a string of module name, and a file_operations structure.

Function invoked while installing the module.

```c
#include <linux/proc_fs.h>
#include <linux/fcntl.h> /* O_ACCMODE
*/
#include <asm/system.h> /* cli(),
*_flags */
#include <asm/uaccess.h> /*
copy_from/to_user */

MODULE_LICENSE("Dual BSD/GPL");

/* Declaration of memory.c functions */
int memory_open(struct inode *inode,
struct file *filp);
int memory_release(struct inode *inode,
struct file *filp);
ssize_t memory_read(struct file *filp,
char *buf, size_t count, loff_t
*f_pos);
ssize_t memory_write(struct file *filp,
char *buf, size_t count, loff_t
*f_pos);
```

```c
int memory_init(void) {
  int result;

  /* Registering device */
  result =
register_chrdev(memory_major,
"memory", &memory_fops);
  if (result < 0) {
    printk(
      "<1>memory: cannot obtain major
number %d\n", memory_major);
    return result;
  }

  /* Allocating memory for the buffer
*/
  memory_buffer = kmalloc(1,
GFP_KERNEL);
  if (!memory_buffer) {
    result = -ENOMEM;
    goto fail;
  }
  memset(memory_buffer, 0, 1);

  printk("<1>Inserting memory
module\n");
  return 0;

  fail:
    memory_exit();
    return result;
}
```

```c
void memory_exit(void) {
  /* Freeing the major number */
  unregister_chrdev(memory_major,
"memory");

  /* Freeing buffer memory */
  if (memory_buffer) {
    kfree(memory_buffer);
  }

  printk("<1>Removing memory
module\n");

}
```

Opening the device as a file:

The memory_open function takes arguments as below:

An inode structure: sends information to the kernel regarding the major number and minor number.

A file structure: Information relative to the different operations that can be performed on a file.

The memory_open function can be seen below:

<memory open> =

```
int memory_open(struct inode *inode,
struct file *filp) {

   /* Success */
   return 0;
}
```

Closing the device as a file:

Function memory_release has as arguments an inode structure and a file structure, just like before.

When a file is closed, it's usually necessary to free the used memory and any variables related to the opening of the device. But, due to the simplicity of this example, none of these operations are defined in open and release functions.

The memory_release function is shown below:

<memory release> =

```
int memory_release(struct inode
*inode, struct file *filp) {

   /* Success */
   return 0;
}
```

Reading the device:

Function memory_read arguments are:

A type file structure.

A buffer (buf) from which the user space function will read.

A counter with the number of bytes to transfer (count).

Position of where to start reading the file (f_pos).

In this simple case, the memory_read function transfers a single byte from the driver buffer (memory_buffer) to user space with the function copy_to_user:

```c
ssize_t memory_read(struct file
*filp, char *buf, size_t count,
loff_t *f_pos) {

  /* Transfering data to user space
*/
  copy_to_user(buf,memory_buffer,1);

  /* Changing reading position as
best suits */
  if (*f_pos == 0) {
    *f_pos+=1;
    return 1;
  } else {
    return 0;
  }
}
```

If reading position is at the beginning of the file, it is increased by one and the number of bytes that have been properly read is given as a return value, 1. If not at the beginning of the file, an end of file (0) is returned since the file only stores one byte.

Writing to a device:

Function memory_write has following arguments: A type file structure; buf,; count, and f_pos, the position to start writing.

The function copy_from_user transfers the data from user space to kernel space.

<memory write> =

```
ssize_t memory_write( struct file
*filp, char *buf,
size_t count, loff_t *f_pos) {

  char *tmp;

  tmp=buf+count-1;

copy_from_user(memory_buffer,tmp,1);
  return 1;
}
```

Complete "memory" driver

By joining all of the previously shown code, the complete driver is achieved:

```
    <memory initial>
    <memory init module>
    <memory exit module>
    <memory open>
    <memory release>
    <memory read>
    <memory write>
```

[Ref: freesoftwaremagazine- Xavier Calbet]

Executing Program:

Compile the previous modules before using makefile.

The module can then be loaded with:

```
# insmod memory.ko
```

It's also convenient to unprotect the device:

```
# chmod 666 /dev/memory
```

Now we will have a device /dev/memory where

we can write a string of characters.

Perform the operation like this:

```
$ echo -n abcdef >/dev/memory
```

To check the content of the device you can use a simple `cat` command:

```
$ cat /dev/memory
```

The stored character will not change until it is overwritten or the module is removed.

Complete Parallel Port driver:

Let's see another example of real driver to perform real task by modifying the driver that we just created. We will use the simple computer parallel port and the driver will be called parlelport.

The parallel port is effectively a device that allows the input and output of digital information. More specifically it has a female D-25 connector with twenty-five pins.

It uses three bytes of memory. In a PC, the base address (the one from the first byte of the device) is usually 0x378. In this basic example, we will use just the first byte.

The connection of the above-mentioned byte with the external connector pins is shown in figure.

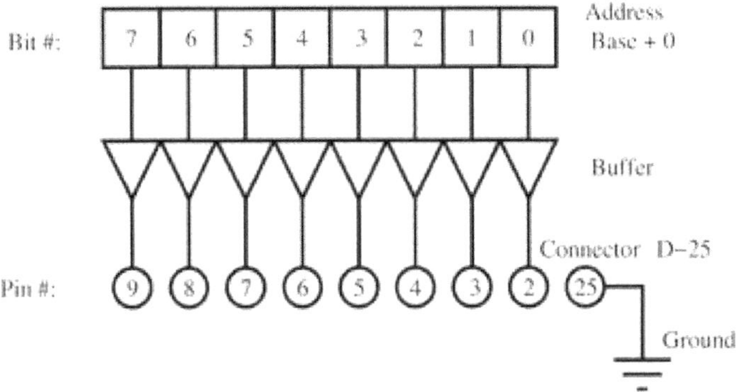

[First byte of the parallel port and its pin connections with the external female D-25 connector]

Initializing the module:

The previous memory_init function needs modification. Need to change the RAM memory allocation for the reservation of the memory address of the parallel port (0x378).

To achieve this, use the function for checking the availability of a memory region (check_region), and the function to reserve the memory region for this device (request_region).

Both have as arguments the base address of the memory region and its length. The request_region function also accepts a string which defines the module.

```
  /* Registering port */
  port = check_region(0x378, 1);
  if (port) {
    printk("<1>parlelport: cannot
reserve 0x378\n");
    result = port;
    goto fail;
  }
  request_region(0x378,
1,"parlelport");
```

Removing the module:

Here it is substituting the freeing of memory with the removal of the reserved memory of the parallel port. This is done by the release_region function, which has the same arguments as check_region.

<parlelport modified exit module> =

```
  /* Make port free! */
  if (!port) {
    release_region(0x378,1);
  }
```

Reading the device:

A real device reading action needs to be added to allow the transfer of information to user space. The inb function achieves this; its arguments are the address of the parallel port and it returns the content of the port.

<parlelport inport> =

```
/* Reading port */
parlelport_buffer = inb(0x378);
```

Writing to the device:

Writing to the device function will transfer later this data to user space.

The function outb accomplishes this; it takes as arguments the content to write in the port and its address.

<parlelport outport> =

```
/* Writing to the port */
outb(parlelport_buffer,0x378);
```

Complete "parlelport" driver:

Now we have to replace the word memory for the word parlelport throughout the code for the memory module.

The final result is shown below:

<parlelport.c> =

```
<parlelport initial>
<parlelport init module>
<parlelport exit module>
<parlelport open>
<parlelport release>
<parlelport read>
<parlelport write>
```

Initial section:

In the initial section of the driver a different major number is used (61). Also, the global variable memory_buffer is changed to port and two more #include lines are added: ioport.h and io.h.

```c
/* Necessary includes for drivers */

#include <linux/init.h>
#include <linux/config.h>
#include <linux/module.h>
#include <linux/kernel.h> /* printk()
*/
#include <linux/slab.h> /* kmalloc()
*/
#include <linux/fs.h> /*
everything... */
#include <linux/errno.h> /* error
codes */
#include <linux/types.h> /* size_t */
#include <linux/proc_fs.h>
#include <linux/fcntl.h> /* O_ACCMODE
*/
#include <linux/ioport.h>
#include <asm/system.h> /* cli(),
*_flags */
#include <asm/uaccess.h> /*
copy_from/to_user */
#include <asm/io.h> /* inb, outb */

MODULE_LICENSE("Dual BSD/GPL");
```

```c
/* Function declaration of
parlelport.c */

int parlelport_open(struct inode
*inode, struct file *filp);
int parlelport_release(struct
inode *inode, struct file *filp);
ssize_t parlelport_read(struct
file *filp, char *buf, size_t
count, loff_t *f_pos);
ssize_t parlelport_write(struct
file *filp, char *buf, size_t
count, loff_t *f_pos);
void parlelport_exit(void);
int parlelport_init(void);

/* Structure that declares the
common */
/* file access fcuntions */

struct file_operations
parlelport_fops = {
  read: parlelport_read,
  write: parlelport_write,
  open: parlelport_open,
  release: parlelport_release
};
```

```c
/* Driver global variables */
/* Major number */
int parlelport_major = 61;

/* Control variable for memory */
/* reservation of the parallel
port*/
int port;

module_init(parlelport_init);
module_exit(parlelport_exit);
```

Module init :

In this module-initializing-routine we will introduce the memory reserve of the parallel port as was described before.

```c
  int parlelport_init(void) {
    int result;

    /* Registering device */
    result =
register_chrdev(parlelport_major,
"parlelport",
        &parlelport_fops);
    if (result < 0) {
      printk(
        "<1>parlelport: cannot obtain
major number %d\n",
        parlelport_major);
      return result;
    }

    <parlelport modified init module>

    printk("<1>Inserting parlelport
module\n");
    return 0;

    fail:
      parlelport_exit();
      return result;
  }
```

Removing the module:

This routine will include the modifications previously mentioned.

```c
void parlelport_exit(void) {

  /* Make major number free! */
  unregister_chrdev(parlelport_major,
"parlelport");

  <parlelport modified exit module>

  printk("<1>Removing parlelport
module\n");
}
```

Opening the device as a file:

This routine is identical to the memory driver.

<parlelport open> =

```c
int parlelport_open(struct  inode
*inode, struct file *filp) {

  /* Success */
  return 0;

}
```

Closing the device as a file:

Again, the match is perfect.

<parlelport release> =

```
int parlelport_release(struct
inode *inode, struct file *filp)
{

  /* Success */
  return 0;
}
```

Reading the device:

The reading function is similar to the memory one with the corresponding modifications to read from the port of a device.

<parlelport read> =

```c
ssize_t parlelport_read(struct file
*filp, char *buf,size_t count, loff_t
*f_pos) {

   /* Buffer to read the device */
   char parlelport_buffer;

   <parlelport inport>

   /* We transfer data to user space */

copy_to_user(buf,&parlelport_buffer,1)
;

   /* We change the reading position as
best suits */
   if (*f_pos == 0) {
     *f_pos+=1;
     return 1;
   } else {
     return 0;
   }
}
```

Writing to the device:

It is analogous to the memory one except for writing to a device.

<parlelport write> =

```c
ssize_t parlelport_write( struct
file *filp, char *buf,
  size_t count, loff_t *f_pos) {

  char *tmp;

  /* Buffer writing to the device */
  char parlelport_buffer;

  tmp=buf+count-1;

copy_from_user(&parlelport_buffer,tm
p,1);

  <parlelport outport>

  return 1;
}
```

LEDs to test the use of the parallel port:

Construction of a piece of hardware that can be used to visualize the state of the parallel port with some simple LEDs.

The circuit to build is shown in figure :

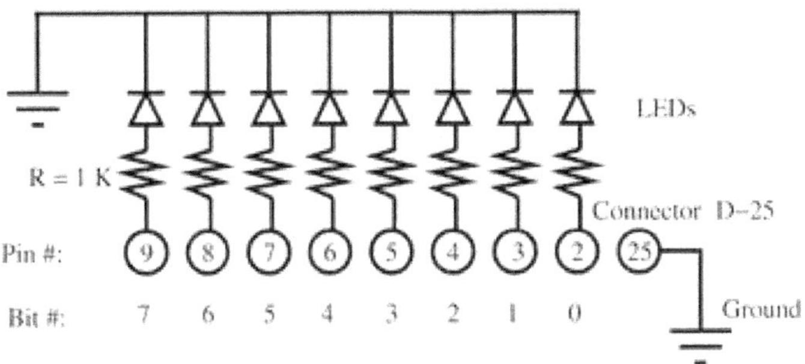

[Electronic diagram of the LED matrix to monitor the parallel port]

First ensure that all hardware is correctly connected. Next, switch off the PC and connect the device to the parallel port. The PC can then be turned on and all device drivers related to the parallel port should be removed (for example: lp, parport, parport_pc, etc.).

The hotplug module of the Debian Sarge distribution is particularly annoying and should be removed.

```
obj-m := nothing.o hello.o
memory.o parlelport.o
```

Create file/dev/parlelport as a root with the command:

```
# mknod /dev/parlelport c 61 0
```

Then it needs to be made readable and writable by anybody with:

```
# chmod 666 /dev/parlelport
```

The module can now be installed, parlelport. You can check that it is effectively reserving the input/output port addresses 0x378 with the command:

```
$ cat /proc/ioports
```

To turn on the LEDs and check that the system is working, execute the command:

```
$ echo -n A >/dev/parlelport
```

This should turn ON LED zero and six, leaving all of the others OFF.

You can check the state of the parallel port issuing the command:

```
$ cat /dev/parlelport
```

Final application: Flashing lights:

Finally, We will develop a pretty application which will make the LEDs flash in succession. To achieve this, a program in user space needs to be written with which only one bit at a time will be written to the/dev/parlelport device.

[Ref: freesoftwaremagazine- Xavier Calbet]

```
#include <stdio.h>
#include <unistd.h></p>

int main() {
  unsigned char byte,dummy;
  FILE * PARLELPORT;

  /* Opening the device parlelport */

PARLELPORT=fopen("/dev/parlelport","w")
;
  /* We remove the buffer from the file
i/o */
  setvbuf(PARLELPORT,&dummy,_IONBF,1);

  /* Initializing the variable to one
*/
  byte=1;

  /* We make an infinite loop */
  while (1) {
    /* Writing to the parallel port */
    /* to turn on a LED */
    printf("Byte value is %d\n",byte);
    fwrite(&byte,1,1,PARLELPORT);
    sleep(1);

    /* Updating the byte value */
    byte<<=1;
    if (byte == 0) byte = 1;
  }

  fclose(PARLELPORT);
}
```

Application can be compiled in the usual way:

```
$ gcc -o lights lights.c
```

It can be executed with the command:

```
$ lights
```

The lights will flash successively one after the other! The flashing LEDs and the Linux computer runs program easily.

You should now be capable of writing your own complete device driver for simple hardware like a relay board.

Chapter 23
Device Driver Debugger

✓ When we load driver and perform some actions on driver developed by us we can observe some system crash and error messages.

✓ Developers can face a problem of incorrect answer or misbehavior of driver. Device driver developers need to solve such problems.

✓ To find root cause of the problem and dig in to code study the behavior of driver debugger is used by developers.

✓ But experience shows that the best debugging technique is using printk function efficiently. By using printk function wisely we can get much useful information about inside of code which helps to tackle the bug.

✓ We can display all important input and output settings and values using printk function and using these values we can get origin of problem.

✓ Once we will be done with the solution of problem then comment out the printk functions. We can hide printk functions used for tracking purpose.

✓ Following tools are used for debugging purpose:

Data Display Debugger: ddd

- Link : http://www.gnu.org/software/ddd/

- Information: This debugger is famous for displaying data structure in graphical format. Tool displays source code and its internal register.

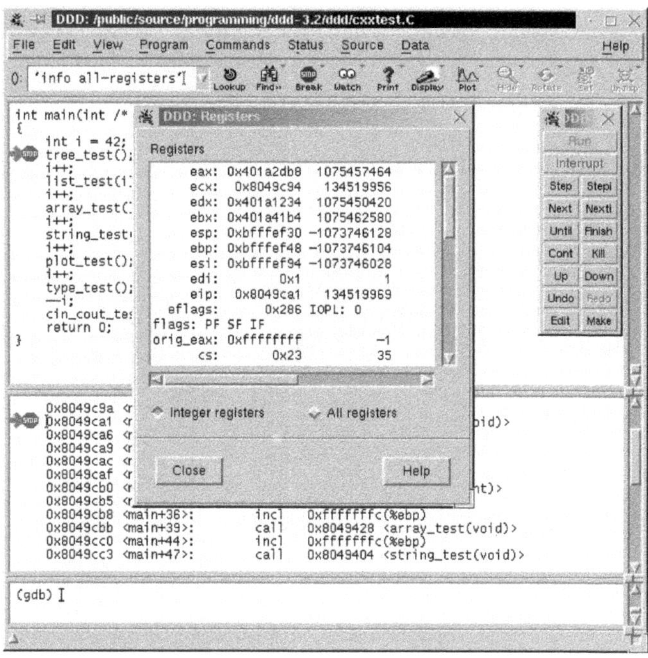

Graphical Display Debugger: gdb

- Link : https://www.gnu.org/software/gdb/

- Information: This debugger is also known as GNU project debugger.

- This is used to see insides of program while program is actually running.

- This debugger can be used for almost all variant of UNIX operating system.

- Here we can stop the program at some condition and observe the exact value changes happened after executing particular condition.

Kernel Graphical Debugger: kgdb

- Link : http://elinux.org/Kgdb

- Information: This is very good tool for kernel debugging.
- Here we can gain complete control on kernel by stop running kernel; also we can perform stepwise execution of running kernel and put breakpoint in kernel.
- We can debug kernel just like we are debugging any application.

- Using above all debugging tools we can perform debugging in very good manner as per our need. But before using these tools we need to configure these debugging tools.
- The best way to learn about these tools is install these debugging tools on our system and whenever we need just start debugger to debug our problem.
- We can gain expertise in using debugging tool by more and more use and experiments on debugging tool.

In this book we started from linux installation and completed all basic things about linux device drivers.

I am sure that this book will be very useful to understand and learn all basic concepts of driver programming in easy and simple way.

After gathering information of all basic device drivers I recommend you to start experimenting and enhancing all device drivers and becomee expert in Linux Device Driver programming.

All the best to become Linux Device driver Geek!

Appendix 1
1] Exported Symbols:

When modules are loaded, they are dynamically linked into the kernel.

As with user-space, dynamically linked binaries can call only into external functions that are explicitly exported for use. In the kernel, this is handled via special directives called EXPORT_ SYMBOL() and EXPORT_SYMBOL_GPL().

Functions that are exported are available for use by modules.The set of kernel symbols that are exported are known as the exported kernel interfaces or even the kernel API.

Exporting a symbol is easy. After the function is declared, it is usually followed by an EXPORT_SYMBOL().

```
int get_pirate_beard_color(void)
{
        return pirate->beard->color;
}
EXPORT_SYMBOL(get_pirate_beard_color);
```

Presuming that get_pirate_beard_color() is also declared in an accessible header file, any module can now access it.

2] Kobjects, Ksets, and Subsystems:

The kobject is the fundamental structure that holds the device model together.

Sysfs is a virtual filesystem that describes the devices known to the system from various viewpoints. By default it is mounted on /sys. The basic building blocks of the hierarchy are kobjects.

A kobject has the type struct kobject; it is defined in <linux/kobject.h>. That file also includes declarations for a number of other structures related to kobjects and, of course, a long list of functions for manipulating them.

A ktype is a type associated with a kobject. The ktype controls what happens when a kobject is no longer referenced and the kobject's default representation in sysfs.

A kset is a group of kobjects all of which are embedded in structures of the same type. The kset is the basic container type for collections of kobjects. Ksets contain their own kobjects.

A subsystem is a collection of ksets which, collectively, make up a major sub-part of the kernel. Subsystems normally correspond to the top-level directories in sysfs.

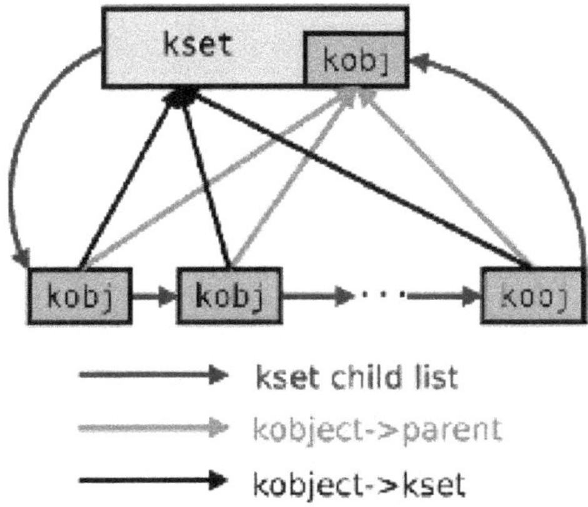

3] DMA I/O:

With DMA, the driver can avoid the time-consuming process of transferring data between memory and device registers.

A DMA device driver has a more complex structure because it must deal with such factors as

- Programming a device to store into a page buffer in physical memory
- Scheduling operations, such as blocking a user process and waking it up when the operation is complete
- Asynchronous interrupts from the device
- The possibility that requests from other processes can occur while the device is operating
- The possibility that a device interrupt can occur while the driver is handling a request

Data transfer can be triggered in two ways: either the software asks for data or the hardware asynchronously pushes data to the system. In first case-

1. When a process calls *read*, the driver method allocates a DMA buffer and instructs the hardware to transfer its data into that buffer. The process is put to sleep.
2. The hardware writes data to the DMA buffer and raises an interrupt when it's done.
3. The interrupt handler gets the input data, acknowledges the interrupt, and awakens the process, which is now able to read data.

The second case comes about when DMA is used asynchronously. Driver should maintain a buffer so that a subsequent *read* call will return all the accumulated data to user space.

1. The hardware raises an interrupt to announce that new data has arrived.

2. The interrupt handler allocates a buffer and
   tells the hardware where to transfer its
   data.
3. The peripheral device writes the data to the
   buffer and raises another interrupt when it's
   done.
4. The handler dispatches the new data, wakes
   any relevant process, and takes care of
   housekeeping.

A device driver using DMA has to talk to
hardware connected to the interface bus, which
uses physical addresses, whereas program
code uses virtual addresses.

Important DMA functions are given in below
table:

#include <linux/dma-mapping.h>	Header file required to define the generic DMA functions.
int dma_set_mask(struct device *dev, u64 mask);	For peripherals that cannot address the full 32-bit range, this function informs the kernel of the addressable range and returns non zero if DMA is possible.
void *dma_alloc_coherent (struct device *dev, size_t size, dma_addr_t *bus_addr, int flag)	Allocate and free coherent DMA mappings for a buffer that will last the lifetime of the driver.
void dma_free_coherent(struct device *dev, size_t size, void *cpuaddr, dma_handle_t bus_addr);	

Bibliography

- Jonathan Corbet, Alessandro Rubini and Greg Kroah-Hartman . Linux Device Drivers,3rd Edition, :O'Relly publications , July 2009.

- Sreekrishanan Vekanteswaran, Essential Linux Device Drivers: Pearson Edition, 2009.

- Jon Masters and Richard Blum, Professional Linux programming: Wiley India Edition,2007.

- John Muster. UNIX made easy, 3rd Edition: New Delhi: Tata McGraw-Hill Edition, 2002.

- Robert Love, Linux Kernel Development 2nd Edition By: Sams Publishing

- Open Source for you Magazine

- Linux For You Magazine.

- Free Software Magazine

- Elektor Magazine

- Internet Guide: Google search, Google images.
- Online Linux Tutorials by Xavier.
- Linux Community website.
- Anil Sir Tutorials and Programs on Internet.
- Wikipedia and all websites related to Linux.

About the Author

Author:

Mr. Mahesh Sambhaji Jadhav

- ➤ Software Industry experience of eleven years.
- ➤ Master of Science in Software Systems, BITS Pilani, India.
- ➤ Bachelor of Engineering in Electronics, Walchand College Sangli, India.
- ➤ Inventor of External Graphics solution.
- ➤ Filed four patents in processor technology area.
- ➤ Author of eight pioneering books.

Contact Information:

- Mobile: +91 9421359187
- E-mail ID: mahesh7197@gmail.com
- Website : www.bolmj.wordpress.com

Vision

"Knowledge across the world should be Open to all, Free of cost, Easy to adopt and should available in our mother tongue." --BOLMJ

Thanking Note

Author would like to thank friends, fans students, teachers to give huge responce to my experiment. It gives motivation to write second edition of the book.

Author will be happy to hear reader's view and suggestions in order to improve the book.

Valuable feedbacks will be useful to enhance user experience of learning EasyLDD in systematic and simple way.

"We highly appreciate the feedback on our books through email, comments on Google play store and ratings on Amazon book store. Thanking in advance for encouragement."

HighTechEasy Publications
Spreading Knowledge

Impacting the world with kind help of ...

Published Books